At home at Belle Lea Acres with his Sidekicks, Ed Karr, Old Pepper, Jay's "Little Lady," and Bob Sievers.

"Hello, World"

being some of the most requested

broadcasts and poems

by

Jay Gould

Farm Service Director
Radio Station WOWO
Fort Wayne, Indiana

FIRST PRINTING — JUNE, 1966

SECOND PRINTING — JULY, 1966

THIRD PRINTING — SEPTEMBER, 1966

FOURTH PRINTING — DECEMBER, 1971

FIFTH PRINTING — NOVEMBER, 1977

Hello World:

It didn't occur to me when we began selecting from the tons of my stuff what would fit best into a little book like this — didn't occur to me that practically all of it that hadn't already been published and copyrighted was written to be read aloud — for broadcast mostly. My rhymes were written to be backed by music in the mood of the thought, and my prose to be delivered in "Voice 18′ so it would come out like I was talking about a foot from your ear.

The second problem was that my advisers wanted me to leave out what seemed to me the best things I had written. They accused me of trying to get published a small edition of *Encyclopædia Brittanica*. After all, thirty-two years of kid stories, Little Doctor Hickory's nature stories, my "Health From the Soil Up" series, as well as a couple of truck loads on agriculture and on my world travels — after all, that's a lot of words.

Anyway, here's what we came up with, and it is my hope and sincere prayer that in this little book you'll find something to inspire you to your own best kind of thinking and toward a little fuller living of LIFE. You see, no thought of mine is really important to you until it has become your own thought or — better still — inspired you to think a better one.

Faithfully yours,

DEDICATION

To the staff of great and good men and women who through the years have molded WOWO into the splendid instrument of service that it is, and for the driving inspiration its power has been to me as it has carried my small contributions to those of you who have listened; this book is humbly and gratefully dedicated.

RADIO NEIGHBORS

I've never seen your face, nor have you mine.

Yet here we sit across the room today;

You so intent on making my heart glad;

And I so willingly invite you stay.

Day after day you sit beside my hearth.

Day after day I bid you welcome there.

Ah, it is good we can be friends like this — —

Can clasp — as neighbors — hands across the air!

MY LIFE I CARRY IN A LEAKY PAIL

My life I carry in a leaky pail,
And drop by drop my hours fall on the sand —
Fall on the thirsty sand and disappear.

Nearer to emptiness, my bucket is
Each step I take. But I must hurry on
Toward my goal far off across the sand!

Must hurry on, too rushed to stop and drink,
Though my thirst tortures me, I must not pause!
Let cracked lips parch! Let tongue grow brittle too!
Let charred throat ache . . . There is no time to waste!
My goal is far . . . My bucket will run dry
Before I reach it . . . I must hurry on!

Dim have my eyes grown . . . Muscles ache for rest —
Lost are the flavors of the food I gulp.
Nor can I still smell fragrance, pungence, stench —
All are the same to me . . . my senses dulled.

Dried is my heart too. Love, a withered leaf.
My goal is far! . . . No dallying for love!
My life I carry in a leaky pail,
My hours are leaking out upon the sand
I must keep on though senses atrophy;
Though heart and soul dry out within my breast.
There's far to go! My thirst must wait! . . . My Goal! !

Drop after drop sinks into thirsty sand . . .
Drop after drop of life — my only life!

A flowerlet smiles a fragrant greeting gay.
But I look straight ahead across the sand.
A friendly tree says, "Stop and rest, my friend,
"Beneath my cooling shade. Refresh yourself."
"But no!" my voice rasps; "I must hurry on.
"My life I carry in a leaky pail!"

Soft gentle hands that I caressed years gone
Reach out and bid me stay awhile for love.
"There is no time!" I cry. "I must go on.
"My goal is yonder, far across the sand!"

A still small voice I hear in kindest tone:
"Son, tarry. There is need for you to pray."
"No! . . . Later! . . . When I reach my goal I'll stop,
"And quench my thirst and love and rest and pray."

A hill . . . a dune of shifting sand I climb.
I reach the summit! Surely there will be
My goal . . . just over there at last I'll see!

"What is it? . . . No! . . . Oh, no! ! . . . A field of bones . . .
"Of whitened sun-baked bones of other men!
"And all around are empty buckets too . . .
"Empty and rusting on the thirsty sand!"

Upon my knees I sink . . . All hope is gone.
But my dim eyes catch writing in the sand;
Words scrawled, I know, by some poor dying hand: —

"There is no goal here, fool, but emptiness!
"But emptiness and death! Your pail is dry!
"He who would live must drink each hour-drop
"From leaky pail in which he carries life.
"For every drop that falls will disappear
"Into the thirsty sand of wasted life."

My life I carry in a leaky pail,
And drop by drop my hours slip away.
Each drop I fail to drink to quench my thirst
Is wasted life lost to the thirsty sand.

BROTHERHOOD

Each thing that *is* in all the world — he is my brother.
The weather beaten rock from which my bones are built,
The microscopic creature in the fertile soil bringing death
back into life,
The hungry root tips searching in the earth to find my food,
The leaves of plants who reach to catch the sun from which
my energy to live, and move and love, must come,
These, each and every one, my brother is.

The rain, the brook, the river, and the sea,
The fish and fowl and insect and the beast,
Each share with me the common blood-line out of Nature's stream.
And men, whatever incidental race or creed,
Whatever politics, or skill, or lack of skill,
Whatever aspiration, hope or fear, or doubt,
All are my brothers — sons of my loving Father, God.

WHAT'S IN A NAME?

How sad that that from which we all are want
To draw, and fill our little cup of joy —
From whose divergent source we each may gain
Fulfillment for our hearts' material wants,
      Should be called "work."

It is the thing we choose above all else,
And to it, give our little train of years,
With only now and then an hour's change
To spend in play — that is — what's not life's choice,
      Or, 'twould be "work."

The happiest man in all the world is he,
Whose lot, from Fortune's hand has been so drawn
That he can find his every wakeful hour
Full and o'erflowing with that blessed joy
      That is called "work."

What harm, I ask, in Adam's awful curse?
Why should we not be thankful, not bowed down?
And on the sweating brows of toiling men
I see my answer writ in lines of pain:
      "God *called* it 'work'."

IN MEMORY OF . . . "PEPPER"

There is Nobody . . . *today* . . . who thinks I'm the greatest man
who ever lived in the world.
But there was yesterday . . .
Old Pepper had to die yesterday afternoon.
He believed it.

Tonight when I go home, there'll be nobody whose heart will almost burst with a shouting, leaping ecstasy of joy at my
coming.
There's Nobody anywhere . . . today, whose greatest satisfaction
is in obeying my commands.

I'm sure he hated to leave us awfully,
Not that he minded so much for himself. But he never seemed to
think that Bob or Mother or I knew how to take care of
things very well.
He always felt responsible to see that we didn't get into trouble.

When he was so weak that he couldn't get off his bed that we had
made for him on the davenport, he became so excited that he
almost lost his control altogether when Mother and Bob
got to crying for fear he wasn't going to get well.
They simply had to laugh and talk happy for his sake.
You see, he felt responsible for them.

Sunday afternoon Bob and I sat beside him. We played "Old
Cat."
When the Old Cat won, that was a score for Pepper.
We laughed and talked jolly and congratulated him each time
he won.
And he smiled all the while and his tired old eyes gleamed with
satisfaction.
Bob and I were happy and all right . . . didn't need to worry
about us.
And he slept much better.
Afterward, when delirium took away his mind's control of his
body, even his muscles had such a habit of unquestioning
obedience that I could calm him by saying "Lie down,
Pepper."
He obeyed my will, as always, rather than his own.

In the late afternoon, when his eyes could no longer see us, he
was calmed and satisfied to have one of Bob's dirty socks
under his nose.

He loved the smell of his family!

After he had gone, and we had laid him on his blanket in the
little coffin we worked together to make for him,

Underneath his nose we left Bob's dirty sock . . . I'm sure he
would have liked that.

A dear friend of ours gave us a root from an old-fashioned lilac
bush a while ago . . .

So we thought old Pepper would like to sleep under that now,
just as he used to,

Some of these days, maybe next summer, its roots will reach
down and touch his great heart, and from his rich love and
magnificent and absolute selflessness will surely flow a
depth of beautiful color . . .

Blossoms lovelier than any other lilacs in the whole world.

And, he will be happy when they bring cheer to us whom he
loved so much.

No, Pepper won't go to Heaven, I'm sure . . .

He probably wouldn't find *me* there . . .

And I'm sure he would much rather be wherever I am than anywhere else.

My lane has suddenly become a dead, lifeless thing of earth and
cinders,

For when I drive in tonight he'll not be waiting there to welcome
me home and to smell me all over to see that everything's
surely all right.

But, Old Pepper isn't gone . . . He's still living in Bobbie, Mother,
and me,

Warming and lighting our hearts with a vision of friendship and
a loyalty that no human heart can ever know. Purifying us
with his teaching of that greater joy that comes with
living for others.

MICHIGAN

Deep within the nation's heartland —
Inland seas forever guarding —
Lies a land of happy living:
Michigan, the "Mighty Mitten."
Wooded hills and verdant valleys
Interlaced with crystal rivers,
Lakes of sky-blue, brooks of silver,
Peopled full with all the wild things —
Deer and bear and fish and pheasants,
Water fowl and nesting song-bird —
    MICHIGAN, THE FRIEND OF NATURE!

Child of seething earth and glacier,
Hiding deep red veins of iron,
Or of salt from ancient oceans,
Oil from great primeval swamp-lands
Pressed ten million years, preparing;
Mountain stumps clawed low by fingers
Of ten million years of North-storms;
Miles of proud sky-sweeping timber
Blending sighing of the pine tree
With the inland oceans' thunder —
    MICHIGAN, THE CHILD OF GIANTS!

And a people full of living —
Seed of pioneer and hunter,
Miner, woodsman, farmer, poet —
Welcoming the sweat of playing
And as well the sweat of labor;
Building strength for world and nation
With the tireless restless vigor
Of a great state — "FRIEND OF NATURE" —
From the land and sky and water
Of a great state — "CHILD OF GIANTS" —
    MICHIGAN, SIRE OF TOMORROW!

METAMORPHOSIS

My soul was so hungry,
So hungry in me,
For the sight of the mountains,
The smell of the sea;

So hungry my soul was
For friends that were fine,
For a house and a garden
That I could call mine;

For one day without worry,
One day without haste,
One day without torture
Of debt to be faced;

So hungry my soul was
To let one day pass
Just lying and dreaming
Alone on the grass

By the brook that skips laughing
Down from the hill,
And creeps on its hands and knees
Under the mill.

So I sought for a pursefull
Of gold, for they said
That would buy me the day
And my soul could be fed.

Year on year, dawn and dark,
I labored for gold,
Till my voice was metallic
And my blood was cold.

At last the day came
When my soul I could nurse;
But I sought it and found
It had turned to a purse.

THEY CALLED HIM DEAD

Into the sea a pebble falls,
And from that pebble tiny ripples move
Across the restless surface of the sea.
On, on and on they roll until at last they reach
Even the farthest shore where the sea ends.
For in the deepest sea
There is no wave begun
That comes to rest.

A friend I loved became a part of me.
And, from his soul rich with the power men know
But never name, I learned to live more richly . . .
(And always understanding is to love.)

Today they told me he had gone away;
That I should never see his face again.
Trembling, they whispered to me, "He is dead."
They wept. But well I knew that it was false;
For well I knew that he was part of me,
And you, and you, and all who called him "friend."
I knew the richness of his soul lives on
In us, to make us stronger men. For that
Same light — his light — is in our eyes today;
And, well I knew that everyone we meet
Will be made stronger for the strength he gave.

What, dead? Not for a thouand years say, "Dead"!
Until the ripple that through me and you,
And you, and all who called him "friend"
Has moved to its most distant shore . . .
Till all the sons of men in all the world
Shall have become more strong;
Because a friend
Lives on in us,
And is *not* dead.

VACATION

Just a rest and a vacation
For the two of us was all —
Just a little relaxation
While the summer turned to fall;

And we camped beside the river
In a little quiet grove.
And we swam and fished a little,
And, we made a little love

In the evening by the fire,
As we sat beneath the sky.
And we heard the songs of insects
From the shadows . . . she and I.

Just a rest and a vacation
For the two of us, was all;
Just a little relaxation
While the summer turned to fall —

But, since then, we have discovered
Something happened by that stream,
For the peace and that communion
Crystalized into a dream.

And, whenever we grow weary
Of our labor or our pain,
We can save ourselves by calling
Up that memory again.

IT'S A LONG ROAD DOWN TO THE SEA

It' a long road down to the sea, lad,
And there is no trail from there —
Only the hills of rolling green,
And the salt wind in your hair.
And there is no grass nor tree, lad,
On the green hills of the sea;
And no place to lie and rest your head
However weary you be.

There's a restlessness there and a roll, lad
A heaving thing, the sea!
The treacherous stars dissolve in rain,
And there is no signal tree.
The valley between the waves, lad,
Is a lonely place to lie;
And a rolling grave you'll find, lad,
When your time shall come to die.

There's a soft wind in the corn, lad,
And the sun is on the hill.
The cattle are coming along the lane.
The wheat is beginning to fill.
Let me put my hand on your arm, lad;
It's strange how tired I've grown —
Too tired to carry on long, lad,
If I should be left alone.

UNCERTAINTY

I see a bud on yonder twig, I think,
And just below it hangs a withered leaf.
I cannot really know that what I see
    Is not a fantasy.

I met a child upon my morning's walk.
She put her hand in mine and listened
While I told her of the happy "nature things."
I showed to her a weathered sparrow's nest.
She asked if they would live in it
    When they came back.

      ● ● ●

I looked for her this evening in the same place.
She was there. But her hair was gray.
And as I took her hand I thought I saw a tear fall.
We walked slowly for we were both tired.
We could not talk;
I felt ashamed to tell her anything.
    She was so wise and still.

We found an empty weathered sparrow's nest.
She asked me why they always had to go away
    And leave the nest alone.

      ● ● ●

I see a child on yonder hill, I think,
And just below, an old man stooped with years.
I cannot really know that what I see
    Is not a fantasy.

I AM A CANDLE BURNING IN THE WIND

I am a candle burning in the wind,
Flickering sickly, struggling in the wind;
Burning one side all up
    As my poor lightless flame
    Withers and melts and hunches me;
    And leaves the unburned and melted wax
    Flow down upon the ground
    To make an ugly pile.

You are in darkness there. Come! Hold me up.
Come shield me with your soft white pink-tipped hand.
Then shall I light your way,
    And all the world's.
    Stars shall I make to glow
    In your soft eyes.
    In my bright light your beauty shall men see
    And God be glorified — for light is God.
I am a candle burning in the wind.
Shield me with your soft hand
Or blow me out.

(After reading the letter, of which the following is an excerpt, I blew a small nasty fuse.)

> *My mother-in-law was a Kentucky farm woman years ago. The oldest of eleven youngsters, and mothered the whole brood.*
> *One day on the farm, she sat rocking with a far away look while I mended the clothes. Finally I asked what she was thinking about, and she answered:*
> *"I always feel sorry for a cow when she is like that — the poor thing doesn't know what she does!" Her red cow Rose was in heat. There was such a depth of human goodness in her moods I never forgot.*
> *Seems to me Henry Luce . . .*

OH, THIS NAUGHTY, NAUGHTY WORLD!

I saw the flowers pushing up their pretty school-girl faces
With brazen impudence at the passers-by.
I heard the frogs in vulgar carousel,
Singing their sensual songs of unbridled passion.
A step beyond, a robin was sporting in abandoned promiscuity
With two males — and she, an expectant mother!

A butterfly decked out in the most tawdry dress
With spangles and cheap jewels,
Was making the most suggestive attempts
To attract the attention of at least a dozen males
Who were hanging around.
Even at the breakfast table,
Two flies repeated their obscene courtship,
With neither grace nor modesty!

I put on my black dress, and hurried away to church,
And thanked God that I was not born a beast,
But was rather of that chosen specie
Whom He made in His own image,
And which knows good from evil!

FATIGUE

Night —
My lamp and me
Imprisoned in a purple velvet dome —

Yellow, uncertain light,
Staggering across a chair, a door,
   A table — bare but for the light's
      Fantastic fingers
      On its
         smooth face.

The white smell
Of cold new linen,
Brittle white pillows — soft like
   smoke —

A tiny foot — body warm — smooth,
   Soft like a kiss —
      Fragrant between my lips
      A strand of stray hair . . .
         Sleep!

MORNING

Across the eastern sky
The Almighty had begun to inscribe
His greeting to the new world.

From his throne
In every farmyard
The regal cock first hinted,
Then commanded
That the re-created countryside awake,
Throw off its downy coverlid of mist,
And bathe itself in the last of the dew
That it might be prepared
To receive the benediction
Of the first rays of the sun —
The sacrament
Of the first song of the morning bird.
A belated owl
Wobbled to his hiding place,
Trembling.

All life lifted up its head
In the turgid realization
That it was part
Of a great unit
That men call God.

But to state the truth:
No man
Was there
To see all this
Except the milkman, who paid no
    attention.

BABY INSOMNIA

I think you ought to go to sleep, you little rascal you,
Instead of making such an awful fuss —
A-kicking and a-crying for an hour like you do!
You'd never guess how painful 'tis to us.

Or, do you know, you little tyrant, that it's like a knife —
Your crying is to mother here and me?
I never heard a noise that could hurt so in my life
As your crying! What's the trouble I can't see.

We've fed you and we've changed you and we've checked for
tummy-ache.
We've rocked you and we've walked you half the night.
Why don't you just shut up and go to sleep, for heaven's
sake?
Your dad is getting mad enough to fight!

Jumpin' crickets! What a temper! — like your mother's
folks, I swear —
Just a howling, screeching, screaming bunch of sin!
You should have a darned good spanking, you unruly little
bear!
If you weren't so small, that's just where I'd begin!

Here, let's dump him in the basket. Let him howl himself
to sleep!
I'll be darned if I can stand it any more!
I'll go down beside the furnace. You can stay up here
and keep
Watch of him outside the bedroom door.

Well! . . . See that! . . . The little rascal got himself all
tired out,
Crying so! Asleep already, see?
Look at that . . . the way he holds his little fist, the lout!
Dog-goned, mother, don't he look like me?

TO MOTHER

From morning till it sets at night,
    The sun is in the sky.
Without it there would be no life,
    Nor light to see it by.

We seldom look up at the sun . . .
    Almost forget it's there.
Our eyes and songs and thanks are giv'n
    To things the sun makes fair.

So, too, the mother reigns supreme
    In our soul's boundless sky;
Our lives, the earth; our loves, the moon;
    Her light, to see them by.

So, for one day, we pause and think
    In gratitude that she . . .
First gave us life, and then, the light
    By which our souls might see.

MY MOTHER'S "ONCE ON A TIME"

"Once on a time," my mother began,
"There lived across the sea
"A beautiful princess with golden hair
"And eyes as blue as could be —

By magic the house and the chairs were gone
For my sisters and brothers and me,
And nothing remained that was real in the world
But my mother's face and her knee.

Across the reaches of time and space
On her soft rich voice we flew —
Away from the facts to but feel and see,
To those dreamed-of things that *are* true.

Castles and palaces — rivers and hills —
Fairies to people the skies —
Golden apples and ginger-bread towns —
We could see through the blue of her eyes.

But, out from the soul of my mother arose,
Like the gentle colors of dawn,
A vision of beautiful thoughts and things
That stayed when the stories were gone.

For, when we awoke from the magic spell
Of my mother's voice and her face;
And the story was done, a glory had filled
The poor little room with a grace —

A grace and a beauty; and each little heart,
As the evening sacrament came,
When each of us kissed the other good-night,
Was warmed with a sacred flame —

A flame, unextinguished by years and by pain,
Forever melting away
The hardened scars where bitterness grows
As the skies and the hair turn gray.

We children have gone now, and left her alone —
For each has his mountain to climb —
But every new step has the beauty and charm
Of a great mother's "Once on a time."

MOTHER "LOVE"

"I love my John so very much,"
    The loving mother sighed,
"I just can't bear to punish him!
    " 'Twould kill me if he cried!

"I see him playing in the road —
    "It's such a lovely place!
"I simply can't say, 'No,' and see
    "Tears on his little face."

And so the "loving" mother let
    Her John play in the street,
Until one day the neighbors came
    And laid down at her feet

A bleeding mass of childish flesh —
    Its day of playing done,
Because a mother "loved" too much
    To discipline her son.

A MOTHER CALLS

You get up, you little rascal!
Come, get up, you lazy girl!
Are you going to lie in bed all day?
Don't you see it's getting lighter,
And your hair is yet to curl?
You can never get to school this way!

Just a good-for-nothing little
Rip Van Winkle's what you are!
Why, hear that! The clock is striking eight!
Well, it's time I heard you wiggle!
Hurry now. It isn't far.
You can dress down here before the grate.

Yes, the house is cold this morning.
I am chilled myself clear through.
And the wind is making such a noise!
Just put on your shoes and stockings.
You can wear your nighty down.
Hurry now, and dress before the boys.

What? . . . No answer? . . . Why, I'm dreaming!
What a silly thing to do!
I'd forgotten that the children were away . . .
Far away, with their own babies.
I am getting old, it's true.
My, it's quiet! . . . Hope they write today!

COOLED

Sweetheart, I took you in my arms tonight
To say "good-bye" before I let you go.
I did not mean the kiss I pressed so hard against your cheek
Should be a token of my love.
Though I loved long and well, yet not, indeed,
Should I before a maiden's feet lay down
Adventure of Life's great experiment.
Something within me whispers, "Youth is here!
"Before you lie steep passes yet to climb —
"Climbed but by men and always . . . men alone."

When, for a moment, warm and fragrant, sweet,
Your softness pressed against me like a dream,
I thought you were the one in all the world
Who could to me be she — the one to love —
To share my road, my life. But now,
The startling coolness of the morning wind
Tempers my mood and warns me to forget
The flame that burned my breast and spurred my heart.
And I recall that all are warm and soft,
And all have kisses sweet for me — or for someone.

FREEDOM

Born of a mighty dream they dreamed — three hundred years ago.
Dreamed in the sceptered monarch's throne; in dungeon dark below;
Dreamed in the clanking galley chains; dreamed in the cloistered
    cell;
Dreamed in the exile's lowly cave; dreamed in the battle's Hell.

A mighty dream of a land where men might live beneath the sky,
Free from the lash in the tyrant's hand, the hate in a tyrant's eye;
A dream of a land where men might dwell as neighbors and as
    friends,
With fear of only the punishment that God and Nature sends.

And, from that dream, America was born beside the sea —
A land of neighbors and of peace — a land where men *are* free —
Free, every one, to stoop or climb; free to be dull or wise;
Free to be blind to what is true; or free to use their eyes;
Free, every man, to labor and as free to waste his day; and, failing,
Free to blame the world . . . the nation . . . or to pray.

Be not deceived! This Freedom to those alone is kind
Who work and think and live life well —
The rest, it leaves behind.
It only gives a man a chance to struggle and to try —
A chance to grow to be a man — for it, perchance, to die.
To you who seek the easy way; who shun the heavy load,
You who dislike to do your share —
Freedom is not your road.

This poem won the 1958 FREEDOM'S FOUNDATION George Washington
Gold Medal Award.

GET MAD

When there ain't nobody loves ye
And the whole darned world goes wrong,
When the song the birds sing to ye
Is the blackest blackbird's song;
When the clouds that you're a hopin'
Will bring some raindrops down
Just fizzle up and let the grass
Turn to a sickly brown;

When the money that ye thought ye had
Ye find's been melted long,
And ye lose friends on the love of whom
Ye'r very life has hung;
When the only one you bank on —
Yerself — has proven false,
And ye find that when the trial comes,
Ye'r own brave manhood halts . . .

Oh, it isn't yer religion
That will save you from a fall
And it isn't yer ability
To simply "smile" at all —
Then "a boy's best friend" can't help ye;
Ye'r too old to call on dad . . .
There's only just one thing to do,
And that's to just GET MAD!

If you can live till Christmas,
You can hang on till July.
And so long as there is life in you,
You simply cannot die.
This world was made for everyone
And you can have your share
If, when old Fate hands you a dud,
You JUST STAND UP AND TEAR!!

OUR LOVE

It was so easy a thing to say
With moonglow in your hair —
Easy to say, "I love you, dear!" —
With romance in the air.

Drunk with a kiss's rosy wine,
Close in the arms of you;
Easy to pledge beneath the stars
To be forever true.

"And do you take this man — this maid —
Until death you shall part?"
Easy to say the words, "I do,"
Love's fever in the heart.

But on tomorrow when we face
The labor and the fears,
And all the pain of broken dreams
That fill so many years —

Then will come words that must be said,
And words we must withhold —
The silver of inspiring words;
The silences of gold.

Then by a glance, a touch, a smile
So deep caresses may
Be given that kisses and "I love"
Compare as children's play.

Then, with my face toward the star
Of our hope, I may stand,
Or struggle on to reach our goal,
Nor pause to touch your hand —

Only to know that you are there
Behind me as I climb —
No greater love could ever be;
For that is love sublime!

A PRAYER

Dear God, You gave me eyes with which to see;
And then You added on a little sense —
Not very much, I know, but just enough
To hint to me the "whither" and the "whence."

And then, by luck, You placed me in a world
Where other folks are much the same as me —
With barely sense enough to make the grade,
And with a pair of eyes apiece to see.

And, God, this may sound foolish now to You.
It may be just that I'm a little queer . . .
But I can't see what good there is to kill
What little sense and sight You gave, with fear.

We're all afraid to look with our own two eyes,
And see what one could see with half our sense.
And then we fear to think of what we see.
Thinking or seeing . . . Is that an offense?

This is a splendid world You gave us, God;
And, best of all, this Western Hemisphere.
Isn't there something, though, that You could do
To save our sense and sight from all this fear?

A few things to those of you who are on the thrilling adventure of growing all the way up.

SHOES

I think 'twould be a splendid thing
If someone would, someday,
Invent a special kind of shoes
That would go on this way:

You'd simply set them on the floor
And put your feet right in,
And they would go down by themselves
Just when you first begin

To put your own shoes on, you know . . .
When you are very small . . .
And, while your feet are close at hand,
Before you grow up tall.

The way they make 'em now, with all
The tongues and straps and strings,
And all the holes to go through wrong
And left and right and things;

Why, it's no wonder, when they've grown
Till they do as they choose,
They just wear pumps, like mother does,
And never fuss with shoes.

THANKS BEFORE FOOD

For joy to work . . .
For strength to play . . .
And love for everyone today; . . .
For eyes to see that all are good . . .
And bodies, hungry for this food . . .
We pause, (as everyone should, dear God.)
And give our thanks to you . . . Amen.

IMAGINATION

We know that frogs and birds and dogs
Can't talk like men and ladies,
And when ducks walk out in the rain
They don't wear coats and wadies.

We know that brownies really do
Not live in shady places,
And that the Lady Moon is never
Dressed in silks and laces.

We really know there are no trolls,
No fairies bright and airy,
Nor Santa Clause with eight reindeers
And gifts and smile so cheery.

When we grow up, we'll try to learn
About the whole creation;
But we shall always love to play
With our imagination.

And so, though we are never fooled
About the fairy stories,
We'll play we are, and love them all,
And have no fear of worries.

THE TEEN-AGE PROBLEM

(Written when I was seventeen and one of them)

"To A Spring Shower"

Whither, from realms of life and fruitfulness unknown,
Whence Spring's awakening alone can come,
Have you, oh carrier of that awakening rain,
Develop'd the power to change me so within?
When from the thickening clouds the shadows fall —
Creep into every corner, writing on the wall
Pictures that no one can understand
Of mating, fruits and grass in a green land
Where Winter sadness, joys, tears, lonely hours
Are changed to magic ointment for the flowers?
Why is it when your wondrous spirits move
I have no way to answer "I, too, love"?
Oh, unjust Nature, why give ME no leaves,
No buds, no roots to answer to your call?
My soul would burst with ecstasy and life,
For there's no outlet in ME for it all!

MY REQUIEM

When I am gone
And the sod has healed over the wound
That I have made in the earth,
Think of me then
As being at perfect rest at last —
Free and at rest.
Think of me free from all the years of pain —
Pain that I suffered with my fellowmen
As we gaze far away with dull eyes
While we are driven
Into slavery and death
By the mighty toys of our own creation.
Think of me
Free from the starvation of my soul
For want of the beauty of sound and line and thought,
Bound from me by cords of commercial silver.
Think of me
Free from the duty
Of joining in the crimes of my generation
In order to feed my children.
Think of me
Free from simulating respect
For those whose ingrown souls
Could be happy in Heaven —
Could sing and feast through eternity
While old friends and neighbors
Were roasting below — in earth or in Hell.
Think of me
Free from the enamel of manners
With which society plasters over its abscessed obscenity.
Think then of the stuff that I am made of,
Dissolving willingly at the tender touch of the root-tips
In the fragrant soil,
And climbing proudly to take its place
In the leaf of a weed or an humble bush,
Where I can look up, at last, without fear or shame,
Into the face of God or of a little child.

THE SNOWFLAKES

The snowflakes are tumbling down out of the sky,
And I am so happy, you see,
For they know of just lots of the pleasantest games
To play with my dolly and me!

We sit side by side by the window and play . . .
My dolly and I do, you know . . .
That the snowflakes are all little actors, and we
Have come down alone to the show.

First, there are the fairies who fly through the sky,
And dance on the air with such grace.
It's easy to see just which one is the queen,
With her jewels and lovely white lace!

Now a horseman rides by, and he gallops up near
To the window; then, hurries away
Over houses and trees with a letter to give
To a lady who's waiting, we play.

And, here come the clowns with their rollicking tricks;
And they tumble and play with each other.
They fall and they bounce . . . but we two have to go
'Way back home to see father and mother.

Then we put on our wraps and we go out of doors
To play hide-and-seek with the snow.
But no matter how well we may hide, they all seem
To find just the right place to go.

Then they tickle our noses and get in our eyes,
And creep down our backs — just for fun!
So we scamper away, but they catch us again,
No matter how fast we may run.

They will laugh with us, dance with us, make our sleds slide,
On the hill that bends down to the creek.
And, although every snowflake is white as can be,
They make roses come right on my cheek.

And, what do you think? When the warm sunshine comes,
They run away fast as can be
Away down in the ground to the roots of the trees
To help them bring Springtime to me.

FIVE YEARS TODAY

Five years ago today I stood beside your mother
While she, torn with such pain as those alone can bear
Who bring into the world new life — new soul — new hope,
Gave you to me.

Now you are by my side, making, with pencil clutched
In play-stained fingers, lop-sided A's and B's;
Working with all your might — each tingling muscle taut —
To do my will.

"What is my will?" my soul cries as you proudly hold
Your paper up and shout, "That's good, isn't it, Dad?"
And when I say, "That's great!" you are so satisfied!
But you are five.

Tomorrow you will bring another page and ask
What is my will. And I shall look at it and know
That I am old — That what of me is you
Must answer then.

And so today, while you are five years old,
I shall not teach you what is good and bad,
But in your sturdy hand place lessons I have learned
Of how to face new days.
For on tomorrow you must face alone
Days that I do not — shall not — understand.

TEN YEARS TODAY

Ten years today in a wonderful world
You've lived and worked and grown;
Ten years of opening ears and eyes
To make that world your own.

For all your eyes can learn to see
And your hands can learn to do,
And whatever your ears can learn to hear
Will always belong to you.

And the souls and things that you touch are yours
And can never be taken away
If your soul and your hands have learned to feel
What they touch along the way.

So, today, my gift to you is the world,
And you shall have it all,
If you learn to feel and hear and see
As your heart and your mind grow tall.

TWO LETTERS

To Scott Hewitt, my God-son, with my gift to him of a Bible:

Dear Scott:

Here is a book for all your life. It is full of mystery and adventure. Here are stories of men and how they went about it to find the world's most precious treasure. Some were wise and some were foolish. Some were quite strong and some were quite weak. Some could see and some were blind. Some could hear very quiet things and some were deaf even to big noises. Here are pages and pages of beauty and song and happiness. Every time you read it you'll be able to hear better and to see better the lovely world that the Lord let you and me live in.

· · ·

To Keith Hewitt, my God-son, with my gift to him of a Bible.

Dear Keith:

If I had my choice of giving to you any ONE thing in the world that I wanted to — just ONE thing, ever — it would be this BOOK. Because every day that you live, you'll like it better and use it more. As you grow older, learn to read it. Learn to find just the story or the song or the lifting thought that you want or need when you take his book in your hands. And you'll find it always fits. For, just as your hands grow, so too will this wonderful BOOK grow.

WHEN WE KIDS PRAY

Sometimes, I think, the grown-ups get
So kind of far away:
So busy with their work and things,
Their profits and their pay,

Their cars and houses and their clubs,
And their society,
And politics, and A.B.C.'s,
Social security —

Sometimes the grown-ups have their thoughts
Full, and away so far
That what we kids are doing, What
WE think and what we are,

And even what we grow to be
So we don't get in dutch
And bring disgrace down on THEIR heads
Is all that matters much.

May be they just don't understand
How much we keep inside.
For they might laugh to really know
The battles that we hide.

May be what happens is that folks
Don't realize that we
Who are just kids, "Just crazy kids"
Who seem so fancy free,

Are really dead in earnest
Though we keep it in the shade
And giggle when we're lonely,
And talk loud when we're afraid . . .

But here is something you SHOULD know,
We kids HAVE loads to bear.
And we, too — almost every one —
Have our own hour of prayer:

For our big brothers and our friends,
Yes, for you grown-ups too.
And when we pray we ask the Lord
To Keep us free and true.

And help us, when tomorrow comes,
To build a better day
Of honor, and of beauty, and of love —
When we kids pray.

HE GOT THE JOB

"It isn't square," I said, "He got the job!"
"He said himself he'd never done the work.
"He had no recommends, and I had three.
"He's only worked odd-hours as drugstore clerk."

So I just waited, and when all were gone,
I asked the boss just why, from all the mob
Of applicants that he had interviewed,
He'd turned us down and given that boy the job.

"No recommends?" he said with pleasant smile.
"I counted eight, at least, while he was here:
"Clean hands — clean nails — clean teeth — and
        clean old shoes;
"He's learned to listen, and his eyes are clear."

"And, most of all, he knew what he could do;
"And wth well-chosen words and calm firm voice
"He showed he was himself — and proud to be.
"And, from those recommends, I made my choice."

A MEMORIAL DAY THOUGHT FOR BOYS & GIRLS

When I was a little boy, we used to call it Decoration Day. Today I guess we call it Memorial Day. But to me it meant taking a long ride, together with my father and mother, and my sisters and brother — a long ride in the double buggy to the little cemetery, where the most wonderful rocks grew in all shapes and colors, and where were scattered lovely flowers and shrubs and the grass was newly cut and soft and fragrant. I never could understand why my mother and father always looked so stern and unhappy as soon as we had passed under the fantastic archway of twisted rusty iron. And then we all trooped across the field, being very careful to keep in the path, until we came and stood by a certain place where my mother and father always shed just one or two quiet tears and my father was always very still and stern looking. And then we'd stand very quietly for a few minutes until my father would say softly, "Well, shall we go now, Mother?" That was the strange melancholy part of the day.

After that we began the holiday, with the most wonderful times listening to stories of all the delightful things that happened when Grandma and Grandad were here. In those days, I'm sure, we didn't know — we children — why it was so. But it was a day of high adventure in the realm of rich memory. And someway through the mysterious alchemy of the years, a thought has grown up from those first Memorial Days of mine — a thought which I'm inclined to believe is a pretty healthy one for boys and girls. May I try to give it to you?

What you and I are, might be called a store of experiences which have been sifted and selected and packed away by our intelligences. That's about what we are. And so when I meet someone and I hear him talk, and see the history of his thoughts, and the outline of his character drawn there — as it's always drawn — on his face, and in the look of his eyes — as I look and listen and feel, *I* experience *him*. And as I experience him, *I* change a little — become a little different than I was before. And then, when I meet someone else, and *their* experience of me becomes a part of *them, they* go along — changed just a little because *they* have met *me* — and each one of the thousands of people *they* will meet in their lives will be changed just a little, because *I* met my friend. Now maybe that's a little involved, but I don't think so.

Let's put it this way: Jim meets George, and so Jim is changed a little. And so all the people whom Jim will ever meet will be changed just a little bit because Jim met George. And then all of the people that Jim's friends meet will be changed a little because their friends met Jim who met George. Do you see the picture?

We *do* live on, not only in the memories of our friends, and in the character of *their* lives. But we also, by our living, change everyone we meet. It's like dropping a pebble in the surface of the sea. The tiny waves roll out — on and on they roll. They meet other waves and change them. And so on and on go the waves that our pebble began until they touch the farthest shore of the sea. Well, it's an inspiring thought — the immortality of personality. In fact, to me it is almost frightening.

It's as true as can be, as I said, that every thought a man thinks, or that a boy or girl thinks — *every* thought that they think makes its mark on their face. And although we may not know it, people can read that story written on our faces. Now, what does this have to do with Memorial Day? The point is, that although our bodies die, and return to the blessed dust from which they sprang, and although our souls depart to realms of bliss or punishment — or wherever you happen to believe that souls go — the ones we love and the ones that impress us, live on here in us. And although our senses of touch and seeing and hearing can't feel them anymore, still . . . within us . . . they are alive and doing, because they are a part of us.

And that's why, boys and girls, when some Memorial Day you stand over the place where *your* mother or father is resting, on that Day you will find within you that of you which is *your* mother or your father — all of the goodness and the bravery and the fearlessness of work and pain — all the gentle kindness and the love of things that are true and clean and beautiful. And you'll wonder then, "Why, oh why, didn't I transplant more of my mother into myself while she was still near me, or of my father, or of that good friend? Why did I let the days slip away — days that can never be recalled?"

And then, on the evening of that Memorial Day, when you have left the place where your mother or father are sleeping, your memory will live over again those days that you are living now. And you're going to ask yourself a question something like this: "I wonder what of me, my friends and children, and my enemies are carrying away with them? I wonder how valuable a part I am becoming to those whose lives touch me?" And the day after that, boys and girls, you will be much better parents, and much better neighbors, and much better citizens. Wait and see.

LEARNING HOW TO LIVE

Learning how to live — to live — surely we will all agree that one meaning of "to live" is simply to survive — to stay alive. This means not only to stay alive as individuals but to keep alive the chain of survival which has been handed down through the thousands of generations through which your ancestors and mine did succeed in staying alive and keeping their bloodlines from dying out. For each one of us represents millions of victors in a million link chain of our ancestry. Shall we say my grandchildren are the last links up to now. Thus far, billions upon billions of competitors have had to lose their lives in competition with our ancestors. And now it's up to us.

If the age of the world were a year, man — *homo sapiens* — appeared here only a few seconds ago. He is the last radically experimental model that old Mother Nature has tried. Many millions of years before him, other animals had tried their hand in the struggle to keep their species alive through the ages. Many of them succeeded, but many of them failed and the history of their failure is written in the rocks. In a great many cases, the reason why they failed is also written there. For one thing, wherever we find in the rocks the sign that any specie of animal has become too highly embellished — has become too fancy —or has surrounded himself with too many unnecessary things, including useless decoration of himself — we may expect to find his race dwindling out in the later rocks that lie above. And unless he gets down to business, we may be sure that Nature, who has no favorites, that Nature will have cancelled his specie from the Book of Living.

It was only a few million years ago that a homely, ungraceful animal appeared which walked awkwardly upright on its two hind legs, and thus left his two front ones free to handle things. And on those two front ones he developed an awkward appendage which we call a "thumb" which worked in opposition to the rest of the appendages on the end of his arm. This made it possible for him to be very much more dextrous — to be able to hold and manipulate things. His eyes were located away around to the front, like the eyes of all the pursuers are. And above them arose a lofty, and loftier, cliff of a brow.

And this human animal that could reason and dream and imagine found himself very fortunate indeed. He was of the homeliest, hairless, thin-skinned, weakest-legged breed; with brittle weak decaying teeth, weak eyes, a nose that could smell very poorly, feet which had to be padded or bound up with the hides of other animals so that they would not be bruised or splayed out into uselessness —

homo sapiens. This human animal could boast nothing in comparison with the dogs and cats and rabbits and horses and fishes and frogs — nothing except that lofty domed skull — survived, because that skull was packed with the gray, wrinkled flesh of a large brain, which could imagine, and dream, and could reason, and could adjust behavior and habits to all kinds of new environments. He was very fortunate indeed. He could live in any climate by manipulating the hides and furs of other animals, and the fibers of plants into protective covering for himself. He could take the rocks, or the earth, or the timber of the trees, or could pack leaves and the grasses into shelter to protect him from the weather or his enemies.

As the years rolled by, by the thousands, we see him using more and more of his superior brain and less and less using his second-rate body. Until, as the years went by, by the thousands, he got so his body could hardly stand anymore — only for a few hours. Most of the time he left the weak thing draped over a frame which he called a "chair." And the muscles of his abdomen relaxed so that, as he got older, he had to hold it on his knees. And he got so his weak legs could hardly carry him. A few miles of walking and he'd be all tired out. By the time he had reached his prime at thirty-five or forty, a few miles of running would kill him. And so he toggled up machinery to haul his weakening body about, to lift him up and down stairs, to float him over the water. He toggled up machinery to walk for him, to read for him, to play his music for him, to write for him, to hammer and saw and plow and wash and iron and sweep — well — to do even most of his thinking for him.

And everywhere he ordered his machinery to sing songs of praise to him for all the wondreful, wonderful achievements which man had succeeded in getting his machinery to do for him. People called it "civilization," "the modern luxury," "a high standard of living," the "forward strides of the human race." And as the years went past he made more and more and more and faster changes in his machinery and kept on calling it "progress" and a higher and higher standard of civilization. He even went so far that he could let machines take care of singing lullabies to his babies, and it was no longer necessary for the mother to tell bedtime stories — (the stories upon which manhood and womanhood have grown since the beginning of man's time). He could command his machine and it would sing thrilling songs of sex backed up by the wonderfully rhythmic clatter of all kinds of hardware. Or he could turn on another machine and, not only let it tell bedtime stories to his growing youngsters, but also show them pictures — beautiful moving pictures of slaughter, and crime, and sin, and sensuality.

Because it kept him so busy earning these machines he no

longer had time to spend training his children, nor did the mother. And so, with their superior minds, they created what was called a "system of education" and hired specialists to do practically all of the work of training for living that parents throughout the ages — all animal parents — have taken care of mostly themselves. But it was a great forward step in progress of *homo sapiens* for two reasons: For one reason so much work was necessary to keep paying for all of the machines that the mother and the father just barely had time to say "Good Morning" and "Good Night" to their children.

But they could leave it up to the great educational system to take care of everything and they didn't need to worry. For another thing; because of the complicated array of machinery that *homo sapiens* manufactured for himself, it was impossible for one parent to know very much about very many of the things. In fact, as the years went by he knew less and less about more and more, and more and more about less and less, so he was pretty much incapable of training his kids.

With this complication in the almost unlimited variation in the things men do to earn what is called "a living," a great change took place in a very important part of life which we call "play." Play, you see, throughout all the generations of all the animals had been a very important part of education, because the young ones used their free hours to do in make-believe, or shall we say in miniature, things that they would be doing when they had grown up — fighting, running, climbing, building houses, killing animals, hunting, and the like. But in this new specialized era of what was called "progress," there wasn't much fun in playing that you soldered the four red wires to the four green posts all day, or that you turned on and off the eight switches on a powerful machine that performed a certain operation on the head of an automobile engine. So new and wondrous kinds of playing were devleoped in which a few dozen of the most physically fit in the school played games with balls and things in magnificent luxurious palaces called "gymnasiums" with marvelously smooth floors — too highly polished to be damaged by just ordinary feet. And all the rest of the boys and the girls thought it great entertaining sport to *sit* and watch these few physically fit and well-exercised ones play their games with balls and things.

To a few of those old-fashioned ones of us who have lived our rough lives close to old Mother Nature, there is still a question if this highly-praised road of progress and this higher standard ot boasted living will prepare our younger generation for living when most of them are denied the good, daily grueling muscle-exercising in the gymnasium or in the field — daily exercise without which no girl or no boy can grow strong, nor completely healthy.

Some of us who have not progressed as rapidly as the rest of the race of *homo sapiens* wonder if our splendid knowledge of conjugation of French verbs, or of the military techniques of ancient generals or with the numerous borrowed rhyme schemes of Longfellow, and the backgrounds of Shakespeare's plays, or even in the exquisite training of scientists in the chemical and physical and electronics and atomic fields, which prepare our offspring to help build vehicles which may take us to the moon, or wipe a nation from the face of the earth — some of us who have lagged so far behind on the road to progress wonder if these things are as important as training a future mother for the simple career of feeding her young ones for complete health with the same scientific completeness that every farmer — *of course* — feeds his cows and his chickens and his pigs.

At graduation time I like to say to the young folks something like this: If education is learning how to live, in the next step in your road to progress you will do well to prepare yourself for the future of your family's race — for the grueling struggle for existnece which you and your children must surely participate in — prepare you and yours for that struggle by biulding strong, healthy bodies, and active clear minds — and there are no active, clear minds outside of active, clean, strong bodies. Otherwise I have my own fears that *homo sapiens* might well lose out to some other specie which has energy and imagination and enough dreams and enough reasoning to prepare itself for the environment in which it must struggle.

Let me paint a picture, if I may — see if you can see it. Here sit two people at a chessboard — playing. The one hidden there in the shadow seems to be an old lady. Her hair is as white as the edge of a summer cloud. Her eyes as blue and soft as the sky between. Her strong old face is as brown as the new-plowed earth, as wrinkled as the mountains and the valleys of the world. Silently she watches her partner's every move. And she herself never, ever makes a mistake. If she takes one of her opponent's chessmen, she always, I think, looks a little sad. But she always takes her winning.

It is you playing there against her. She is old Mother Nature. And it is she that never breaks one of the rules of the game. The chessmen there before you are the truths of nature — of the world and of the universe. Whether you like it or not, my son, you have to play that game with her. You have to play against a perfectly honest, calm, just opponent who is glad if you win. But who never overlooks a single mistake—who doesn't ever make the tiniest allowance for your ignorance of the rules, and who never, ever gives you a chance to change your mind once you have made a move. You and every living creature in the world must play this game with old Mother Nature all your lives.

Do you see the picture? Do you? Schools and education are designed as the castles on your chessboard — their function was never to appease politicians, to distribute propaganda, to have to stoop to sell their product to the ignorant materialistic selfish mobs. Education is the learning of the rules of the mighty game of life which you and I have already begun to play. The fittest, we call the winners—and the rules include not merely the knowledge of things and of forces—not only an understanding of men and their ways, not only the methods of ruling your own mind and your own will and your own affections and your own fears — but also the development of a passionate desire and joy in moving in harmony with the rules of the mighty game. That is what education is. You have now begun yours. And anything short of it, anything besides learning the rules of life is not education.

Education never stops except for fools. Your real education will come outside of the schoolroom, and far from the textbooks in your high school or your university. It will come in this great University of Living. And the main thing you can hope to get from your school days there behind you, or those ahead of you — the main thing is to learn how to get educated in the University of Life — to learn how to escape the punishment that will always come from a disobedience of a natural law — the rule of the mighty game, and to learn how to capture the reward which always — always comes to those who play according to the rules.

Your history, your science, your mathematics, your languages — most of the facts of them you will forget before you have any use for them. But what you will keep to use to win by, if you win, will be the ability to look upon the history of tomorrow and today with the same clear overall vision that you should have learned in your school — to know how to look at facts coldly and honestly as your science has taught you — to develop the ability to arrive at a conclusion by clear concentrated thought like that you exercised in your arithmetic and algebra and geometry — the ability to say or write what you think and feel, and to read or hear what others think and feel as you should have learned to do in your language classes.

Almost every living thing in the world hopes that you will fail. And old Mother Nature herself doesn't care at all. She would be just as happy if *homo sapiens* failed and took his place in history beside the extinct archeopteryx, the sabre-toothed tiger and the dinosaur — just as satisfied if they failed and the insects took over (as they may very well do some of these days). Living is a great, and a wonderful, and a thrilling challenging adventure. And besides, there isn't anything I've found that is half so much fun.

WELL, WHAT IS LIVING?

The word live isn't a very good one. It's a little too much like the old cheap monkey wrenches we used to use when I was a kid on the farm. You could screw them out or in so they would fit almost anything. But they just never would fit well enough so that they'd stand a very hard pull. In the previous chapter we talked about living from the standpoint of just staying alive or surviving. You as an individual, as the last link in the chain of your family race, and also all of us as the last links in the great chain of the animal called *homo sapiens.* But there are degrees, I think, of living. And the best way I know of to pass the thought across from my mind, to your mind, is to tell you the story of two people that I know.

A few weeks ago I had the opportunity of talking to a man who said he was a hundred years old. It was my first experience with a conversation with so old a person, and all day I looked forward to the questions I wanted to ask him — what he saw in these changing days. And most of all, now that he could look back over a hundred years, to find what to him seemed most worthwhile in the world, and also, of course, what wasn't worthwhile. But it was a great disappointment. The old gentleman's mind seemed very clear, and his memory remarkably fresh. But in all those 100 years he really hadn't lived so very much at all. Now here is what I mean — life can't very well be measured by linear measure, that is, by inches and feet and miles or years.

It must be measured by cubic — by three dimensional measure — by length, by breadth, and by depth. Its length, to be sure, we call years. Its breadth — well, one's intelligence, one's ability to think and to see, to comprehend and understand the world through which he is passing. One's ability to weigh the relative meanings of things. That is the breadth of living. And the depth — the emotional dimension of our lives — our loves, our artistic expression in music or any of the forms of art, surely the art of making a home lovely, surely in religion, surely in patriotism. Yes. that old centenarian with all his 100 years of living — shall we say a hundred feet long — he had no loves to speak of, no religion worth mentioning, no patriotism worth a personal sacrifice. His life was only an inch deep. And it gave you a tired, dazed feeling to realize how very, very little he had actually thought — how little he had actually seen or understood as he passed through all his days down through life. His breadth was only one inch. So, if you follow my little whimsical arithmetic, the measure of his life was one inch, by one inch, by 100 feet. I figure that 1200 cubic inches. Don't you?

But I also know so many folks, **and** so do you, who live full rich days. Take my good friend Aunt Mary. She is 50 years old. That's 50 feet, isn't it? But in the depth of her life — well, she has five living children and several grandchildren. And she suffered with loving kindness beside the bed of a sick one until he had to go away. She loves boys and girls. She love sher flower garden, and she loves the birds which she feeds all winter long. She has been a good worker in her church. She has many close and precious friends and neighbors who are dear to her. And she is fond o fmusic. She still plays and sings. And she is deeply American. In other words, Aunt Mary's life is deep. Shall we say, ten feet deep?

And her life is broad, too. She can talk politics, and government (sometimes quite a difference). She is interested in economics. She will visit with you about labor problems or international affairs. with just as much vivacity as she can in discussing canning and gardening, making quilts or raising chickens. And she has woven together the threads of experience and of facts and of her thoughts into a pretty clear pattern which you might call a satisfying philosophy of life. Shall we say Aunt Mary's life is 10 feet wide?

Well, when we multiply out her life's volume — 10 feet by 10 feet by only 50 feet, we find that Aunt Mary at 50 has lived a volume of 8,640,000 cubic inches. And that man, twice as old — only 1200. Well, it is not very scientific, I know. But somewhere in among these figures there's a story of the enormous difference in our lives in how much we really do live as the years go by.

It was that great, modern prophet H. G. Wells who said: "Civilization is the race between education and catastrophe." And if you agree with me that education is LEARNING HOW TO LIVE — if you agree with me that surely one part of that task of learning how to live beside that of building and keeping our health for a long life — is developing an emotional depth to our life's dimension — and a broadening of vision and comprehension, then I hope you'll also agree with me that there is another task. That is to learn the rules of the game of prseent day economics so that we can have enough of that necessary evil — money — enough to make the development of these three great dimensions possible. For surely without money you can't pay the exhorbitant costs that are demanded by this great boasted "civilization" which we have attained by this road which we have called "progress."

MENTAL HEALTH AND SELF-OBEDIENCE

I've seen it all happen during my lifetime. It started early, right after the turn of the century, this new thinking about the raising of children . . . started at about the same time as the phonograph, the telephone, the automobile, the building of municipal communities around manufacturing centers, and all of the frightful and world-shaking changes that came to us as chemistry, and electronics, and mechanics took over to rule our lives, where before it was mostly "nature" . . . the air, and the sun, and the rain, and the sky . . . plants and animals and soil. The world is all right! It's simply that our change of environment has been too much for us all. It isn't possible for any one generation to go through the cataclysm of change like we have had in the last century . . . impossible to go through it without enormous casualties in our mental, as well as our physical health, in our philosophies of living, in our religion, in our homes. The change in our ideas about child rearing came as a part of the re-adjustment to city living, I think, and away from farm living; and also, as an adjustment to our new communication . . . the radio and television, and the telephone . . . and rapid transportation which can get us away from home so very easily.

The farm wife with her big family, and all the work that needed to be done not only in the house but also out of doors, had every hour of her day filled with things to do that meant something, and the children had to fit in; first of all, by staying out from under foot and staying out of trouble; and then, as soon as it was possible, to pitch in and do their share of the work. When most of farming and home-making was by hand or by animal power, a boy or girl of five was capable of coming very close to earning their own living by the actual work they did in the home. And if the boy didn't get his jobs done right, he got his britches warmed, genuinely, promptly, and without very much philosophizing.

At school, as well as in the home, good, sound, and very real physical punishment was accepted as a part of good child-rearing. Just as it is in almost all of nature; surely the cat and the dog, the pig and the chicken . . . the bear and the lion . . . and all, discipline their young with vigor, and the same generosity that they exhibit in their gentle and loving care. I was just entering the teaching profession myself, at the very high tide of this new namby-pamby attitude toward rearing a child, when it flooded the minds of almost everyone who was "up-to-date" in America. We were supposed to molly-coddle them along, to let them do it their own way, to let them do as they pleased, to *explain* to them *all* of the reasons why they should do this, and shouldn't do that, and never by any means do more maybe than lightly tap their little bottoms. And I can tell you now, that in my opinion, the last thirty years we have been doing the best we could as educators, as well as parents . . . the best we could to develop soft weaklings, who are unhappy if they have to work, who have lost the joy of conflict, who cry to be given the pablum of security, who have lost one of the essentials of happy manhood and womanhood, and that is rugged, substantial, and surely, unflinching *self*-discipline.

This life is not all soft cushions and dessert, and it surely isn't all love and security. No one can give security. It must be earned. For those who succeed in living it, this life's a tough one, and that's why it is fun. It requires labor . . . hard labor . . . for every single body, all their life . . . hard labor and the *joy* of hard labor. Otherwise, without the *joy* of labor, we cannot achieve mental health, nor physical health. In fact, otherwise, I don't think we can really achieve. It's poppycock that boys and girls should always have the reason *why* explained to them. There are just some things that ought to be done, and that's it! There are plenty of things that need to be explained, to be sure, as the days go by, but in the meantime, children need a pretty unbending code of behavior, without worrying too much about "why."

There are some things you just don't do. You don't steal. I don't really know even yet of any very good way of explaining why not to steal. It isn't quite clear to me what the difference is between stealing $10 from you, or charging you $20 for a $10 article. But you just don't steal, period! And that's all there is to it. And you *work* . . . *You get your* job done as it should be done, when it should be done, *whether you like it* or not, whether it's washing the dishes, hanging up your clothes, sweeping the floor, raking the lawn, or any other job.

It is my impression that during the last thirty years we have *trained* our boys and girls to search for ways of getting out of these completely essential self-disciplines . . . essential disciplines to be happy, in fact, if they are going to be *free*. Because the tap root of freedom . . . and don't forget it . . . the tap root of freedom is *self*-discipline. And a part of that self-discipline is the development of good habit paths. I might add, that in my opinion at least 25% of the disastrous tensions and pressures under which our mis-trained; our untrained, boys and girls suffer today . . . at least 25% of those tensions and pressures would be eliminated if they had first developed an unquestioning acceptance of the essential habit paths of "thou shalt not" as well as "thou shalt."

Here is a boy whose mother has to *remind* him every morning to wash up clean before he goes to school. Lucky is his neighbor boy who has been trained long before school started . . . been trained in the absolute *habit* of cleanliness, of combing his hair, of cleaning his teeth, of bathing, of scrubbing his hands . . . yes, and his wrists . . . and up behind his ears. And happy is the boy who has been trained that doing a job right and on time is an imperative *habit*. Here is happiness, here is peace, here is relaxation, here is fun in living, here is inspiration to achieve based upon habit and self-discipline, as over against the first boy tortured with confusion and tension, self-dissatisfaction, frustration; who makes every day of his life a conflict, as he goes about it to see what he can get away with, without getting into trouble.

We see the tragedy all about us in gluttony; people who eat to excess, drink to excess, play to excess, who are intemperate in listening to the radio, at looking at television, in reading, buying clothes, or smoking . . . and a thousand other ways. These may well be the same people whose mothers had to hide the candy or the cookies, who stuffed themselves with sweets and goodies between meals, who suffered with food finickynesses, and who were not trained to go to bed at night without fuss or furor.

Let us go back to the child for a moment or two and see if we can follow some of these disciplines, or lack of disciplines, along up through life. Here is a young mother, completely unprepared for marriage, and surely for parenthood, because her education has typically left out most of the things that she will actually need to know in her career as a wife and mother. Then she has her baby. It's a new and frightening and wonderful world for her, and her child becomes an outlet whereby she may lavish her emotional confusions, blended in with the joys and the flaming hopes of young motherhood. Without much thinking, what she wants to do most is to give to her child love and security. She feels like submitting to every whim; she doesn't want to hear the baby cry, and as he grows older, she uses the counterfeit money of fondling and pampering as the purchase price of his silence and of peace for herself. And this child, not learning the essential lesson that in this world you can't have everything you want, no matter how loud you may squall, becomes his mother's tyrant and she his slave. And the next inevitable step . . . those who fail to give him what he wants when he wants it, including his father, are mean to him.

And then this unprepared mother sends her child to school and it's too late. He gets into a little trouble, and she comes into my office. He'll sit very close to her because she stands for protection and security to him. And she'll fondle and maul him and caress him while you're trying to discuss the problem. And 99 times out of 100 she'll spend most of *her* time trying to make excuses, trying to get you to believe a false story in order to protect her child from the important and necessary job of facing the music.

In real life we must face the music if we are to be good citizens. It was Solomon who said: "Withhold not correction from the child," and then he added, "If thou beatest him with the rod, he shall not die." If a switch is needed to help a child find his way to obedience and self-discipline, there is no better way for a mother or a dad to express their genuine love, which includes . . . and I know . . . a very genuine personal suffering, this inflicting pain upon someone you love so much. But if we are to succeed in helping our boys and girls grow up to the full stature of maturity of mind and the satisfaction and happiness that comes from a realistic adjustment to the world in which they must live, then there is no greater contribution we can give to them than helping them to build a very stong and tough framework of the right habits, of relentless self-discipline, of things that you just *don't* do, and that's all there is to it; and of things that you just *do* do, and that's all there is to that. The tensions, the pressures, the confuion, the frustrations which are taking such a frightful toll in mental illness cannot be comprehended. It is the greatest single health problem in America today, and I think I have given you one of the answers.

It's a great and wonderful old world. It's a tough one, full of very real challenges for the best a man has in him, and cruel to the softling. And the courage and determination with which one is able to meet the world's challenges is built, from babyhood, out of this stuff of realism and toughness and ambition and responsibility, and surely a lot of unflinching self-discipline.

You don't learn to play ball sitting under a tree. You don't learn to fight looking at television (and that isn't the way to fight, anyway); you learn to sing by singing, not by running a record player. And Mother, the first few years of our lives is the time we learn best about how to live, and unquestioned obedience to one's own best self is the best way to live.

NEW YEAR'S

Here are some of the thoughts that have been going through my head as the old year died and the new one was born this morning.

I was going to exclaim about the gigantic strides of progress we are making in science — the successful conquest of the un-dreamed power within the infinitesimal atom, which in itself is a tiny solar system; the forward push of automation which is so rapidly replacing, not only the labor of man's muscles, but also ot men's minds. One of my discarded scripts started out to sing the praises of the upsurge in agricultural technology which is bringing to pass production potentials of food and fibre and — we mustn't omit narcotics — production potentials almost beyond comprehen-sion. The phenomenal conquest of speed and space and the universe which my generation has achieved, was another subject I consid-ered "taking off" on.

But each time other thoughts came in to warp the story I tried to tell: The question, "What are we doing? Where are we going? Where do we want to go? Why? Is this good? Is this bad? Why? What is important? Where ARE we? . . . Where ARE we?"

You see when you try to find answers to these questions you have to get back down to a foundation thought to start with . . . back down to the UNIT from which to build a thought. And as I thought it through — this far through — I couldn't find any Fun-damental except that of the good of man as the test of the suc-cess of any change . . . or lack of change or condition.

Let me give you a sample of my confusion . . . They say busi-ness is going to be good this year. What is business? Well, I guess you'd say it's the production of things or services and then the entire process of moving those things or services to the one who buys those things. Now let's take that back to the test-unit. THE GOOD OF MAN . . . *A* man . . . And all men. *A* man produces a lot of something that others want. He makes a good income. That's good! . . . Well, now wait a minute. That income is money . . . He uses it to buy things. That's good! Well, now wait a minute. That *does* give employment to others who can make money and so buy things and services, so others can . . . and others and others. That's good! Well, now wait a minute. "Well," you say. "Why wait a minute? Everybody benefits by increasing the goods and services they can accumulate. There's no argument about that," you say. "That's why we have the highest standard of living of any nation in the world — by having more things and services than other people have." And if I repeat "Now wait a minute," you'll probably say "turn that dial, that Jay Gould is surely off his rocker."

But, you see, it's not clear to me, I guess, just what a high standard of living IS for a MAN. Is it having everything he wants?

Standard of living — What is living anyway? Yes, things and services are part of living, I guess. I'd ask first for a good healthy complete body, robust and energetic enough to get fun out of work, and have plenty left for thinking and playing and asking questions about EVERYTHING . . . That takes energy, you know. I'd want to be a good dad, a good lover, a good neighbor, a good citizen. You have to be living to be that kind of a man. And I'd like to be balanced — balanced with an interest in and an understanding of all the things that are going on around me. If having all the things and services is living — a high standard of living — my hogs are hams and shoulders ahead of me. But they comprehend nothing but their own needs and desires, have no interest in anything except their own needs and desires . . . Think it over . . . and maybe you'll say . . . "Jay, *you* wait a minute while we ARE thinking it over."

Each year of my life more and more attention has been focused on food, clothing, housing, luxuries . . . as the things most desirable . . . "the necessities of life," we called them. Things and services, first of all to keep from dying — food and clothing and shelter . . . And then, as we progressed, the luxuries too . . . Well, I can't just remember what some of luxuries DO do . . . They . . . a . . . a . . . they save me labor so I don't have to use my muscles, in fact, don't need muscles. Isn't that wonderful, or IS it? I am so rich I can put fancy furniture in my house to . . . to . . . to impress you . . . to show off, I guess. But when I think of it again, if my furniture makes any difference between you and me, I don't think I like you anyway.

I drive up to your place in my fancy new car. You compliment me on what a beauty it is. And that makes me proud. Well now, after all I didn't design its loveliness or fanciness. I didn't make it. I don't even know what makes it go so wonderfully. All I did really was to labor away at my job . . . my production of goods or services. And then, when I got paid, I spent my money for this car instead of for something else. Now that I think of it, I don't know for sure how proud I am that my car is fancier than yours. In fact I'm inclined to think that if it makes a darned BIT of difference between you and me what kind of vehicle I use for hauling my weak body around in . . . I don't like you anyway.

I might have used my extra money for buying a record player that would make noises of one kind or another around my house or would bring me the music I hadn't taken the time to learn to make for myself — too busy making money so that I could buy things and services . . . Or a machine with pictures to lead my thoughts around like a bridled horse, because I'd concentrated so much of my energy and attention on my production of things and services — on my job — that I hadn't enough left to generate MY OWN thoughts and their directions. And beside my specialized job in this wonderfully progressive world of automation and high production doesn't give me much of a chance to study and observe and question all the things that are going on around me . . . Not much of a chance to collect the ideas and experiences from which full rounded-out thoughts are built.

Let's say I am an expert in running this amazing new and complicated machine which fastens together two parts of an automobile. But I didn't make the machine. I couldn't build an automobile. In fact, as a modern man in this modern world of specialization and automation and science and what they call "progress," there isn't much of anything at all that I can do except run this amazing machine so very well.

Lewis Mumford, one of the world's great thinkers, put it pretty harshly when he said, "We have created an industrial order geared to automatism, where feeble-mindedness, native or acquired, is necessary for docile productivity in the factory; and where a pervasive neurosis is the final gift of the meaningless life that issues forth at the other end. More and more our life has been governed by specialists who know too little of what lies outside their province to be able to know about what takes place within it; unbalanced men who have made a madness out of their method." What are we aiming at, to produce men or products?

I'm starting out this new year completely confused. I'm questioning everything that *before* I have taken for granted to be progress toward the good goal. If it is not good for MEN — complete balanced men, it's not good. And as our nation faces up to a life and death competition with nations who build their technological progress on soul-less, cripple-minded robot-men, there is but one hope. And it is the greatest test in all the history of mankind. Can we or can't we produce complete men balanced in living? If not . . . why bother? And surely, why boast?

Holidays have always been a challenge to me to bring to my listeners thoughts that are a little special and different.

WASHINGTON'S BIRTHDAY

Today our story is about a certain brown-haired, blue-eyed, large-headed, long-armed man — a tall, silent, cold-eyed gentleman . . . Six feet three inches tall he was . . . The son of one Mary Ball, second wife of a Virginia farmer named Augustine Washington. But our story will not be so much about this *man* George Washington whose stony, passionless, firm-jawed stare has chilled the school rooms of America for over 200 years. We shall make no repetitions of the story of his honesty, which was always so discouraging to me when I was hearing them the first sixty-five hundred times. And I doubt if we would get so much of an adventure in reiterating this stuff with which smart-alecks used to try to thrill me about George Washington's slave holdings, his ill tempers because of bad teeth and stomach, and his home-made false teeth; nor of his ability to throw silver dollars across narrow rivers, to chop down his father's cherry tree, or to over-ride his pony.

A few days ago you and I celebrated the birth of the one who held together and tried to repair the rotten framework of our nation's unity, after its timbers had been eaten away from within by the termites of selfishness and greed — Abraham Lincoln — the American with a heart. Today we are remembering the one who silently, and with clenched teeth and brawny arm, hewed out of the tough knotty oak of the colonial wilderness those very timbers for the framework of our nation — George Washington — the American with a mind.

Let us paint a picture: Here in the center, a cold-eyed, fearless, careful mind — a mathematical mind — a mind which could lead a handful of untrained, unequipped, unpaid farmers through eight years of heartbreaking defeats and runnings away — who could face the British masters of the world with an army never larger than 18,000 in a single battle and by the end of those eight years, could wrest from their iron fists the possession of a pretty valuable part of their powerful Empire, with a little army of — yes — at the last — with an army of only 6,000 men. Here was a man who could bid a fond farewell to his weeping, worshipful officers when the peace had been secured and then, within the hour, start for Annapolis to render the exact account of the expense of the Revolutionary War. In his own handwriting, and correct to the cent — $74,485 and some cents — the price of Independence — $74,485 and some cents.

A great world war had just come to its end after seven horrible years. George Washington was 31 years old. France, Austria, Russia, England, Germany, Sweden, Spain — all of Europe — and all of Europe's colonies has been affected. Up to this time, it was all right with England so long as her colonies of the new Western world stayed out of too great trouble and continued to send their raw materials to the mother country and to buy their goods there. But now there was a thought of Empire — of power. And with some two or three hundred thousand Indians and some 85,000 Frenchmen — hateful and smarting with their defeat — England would have been pretty foolish, don't you think, to have trusted the disunited colonists to protect themselves and their land; that is, if this great land was to be held as part of the British Empire. Some 20,000 British soldiers had to be sent to protect the colonies from the French and the Indians. And now that the war was over, 10,000 didn't seem too many to leave here to police them.

That would have been perfectly all right with everyone. And the colonists surely would have been willing to help support these British protectors. But somehting had happened to the mind of the world. For one thing, such phrases as "Liberty, Equality, Fraternity" — "The Rights of Man" — "Individual Liberty" — such words had begun to take hold on people's minds all over the world.

That was one thing. And there was another thing: During war times a great many people make quite a little money. Times are good. And when times are good people go in debt, and they get the idea of living very high. Manufacturers gamble with enormous profits from the production of necessary war materials, to be paid for from their very own neighbor's taxes. And that kind of thing happened in the colonies of America when Washington was about thirty-one years old.

Then the bloody, poisonous bubble of war prosperity broke. Debts could not be paid. Taxes were too high. People could not buy. And people could not sell.

Now far back in *those* days men were a little stupid too, sometimes. And instead of understanding what was the trouble, they acted like babies. They cried and stamped their feet and kicked the table legs and shook their fists at the first thing that they could see. They didn't have a Secretary of Agriculture nor of State to blame it on or a Republican or Democratic government. But they did have an England. And so England became the "goat." They couldn't see any reason why they had to pay their taxes to help support the British soldiers. They couldn't see why they were forbidden to strike out across the mountains in the Indian hunting ground, where they would need even *more* soldiers to protect them. And they could not understand why they should be asked to pay their share of the government costs without having a representative in Parliament. But the British, on the other hand, could not realize what the generations of hardy tough living in their struggle with the forces of nature, had done to make men independent and stubborn and distrustful. And, last of all, the English did not realize what masters of trouble making had come up to plot revolution in America — fanatical, narrow-minded bull-headed haters like Samuel Adams and Patrick Henry.

As we look at it now, we can't see so very much evidence of all that tyranny which the orators of Washington's time made so very much noise about. And I don't suppose — if we had had more history before that time, and more oratory — I don't suppose we'd have had so much fun for so many years "hating" the "British tyrants." And I suppose there would have been some other and better orations for the poor school boys to learn — the school boys who for cneturies have strained their *shrill* voices hurling defiance across the sea at the sleeping ashes of that poor old fool of a king, George I. In fact, organizations still exist today who insist upon beating those same tattered drums.

But, from a close hand view, there was nothing to be laughed at. Distrust was the theme of the day — distrust and dissatisfaction. Thirteen separate little nations, each distrusting the other and each divided within itself between the poor and the rich. The great social unrest, which had swept to America across the Atlantic from the East, left the poor classes more and more conscious of what they were missing of the luxuries of the times. And the times became more and more unsettled. Even as late as 1776, the people of the colonies were having as much trouble among themselves — yes, more — than they were with the British. Mobbings, lynchings, burnings, destruction, and confiscation of the property of wealthy conservatives, became so common that singly or in groups they left the country. From eighty to one hundred thousand of those representing the wealth and culture and conservative careful thought fled the country. The days of possible, thoughtful and careful counsel between the English and the colonists were past. It was a heyday for the *passion*-lashing orators.

Now it is one thing to shout in sonorous gusto: "Give me liberty or give me death" — to bellow cyclones of words about the "rights of man." But it was quite another to build an army with no government behind you — with no money, no nation, no unity — to train that army to meet the world's most powerful nation. That is a different thing. But a different one yet is to hold together a fighting forces of that army through over eight years of almost continuous defeat — through starvation, privation, heart break, defeat, and with no power to keep a soldier from walking off home — no power except the silent grandeur of a steel-jawed tall man.

Compared with that manly silence of George Washington, and his almost super-human deeds there comes a tinny ring to the ranting of Samuel Adams and even to the gallant "Give me liberty or give me death" of Patrick Henry, whose oratory has almost drowned out of our history — another thoughtful, quiet gentleman — a young printer — the son of a soap maker. His name, Benjamin Franklin. And he has been almost forgotten as another one of the saviours of the American Independence.

And there you have the background — a background of selfishness and greed and meanness and stupidity. And against that background, six feet and three inches of silent manhood which could make a disunited people win their independence in spite of themselves and who hewed out of their knarled and knotty stubbornness the oak timbers of a *United* States.

LINCOLN'S BIRTHDAY

The twelfth day of February — the birthday of another man whose birth place was lowly and humble and who sprang from the lowly and the humble of the world's society. The First Divine Lover of the men God had made said, "Blessed are the poor, for they shall inherit the earth." This second immortal lover of men said, "God must have loved the common people because He made so many of them." Abraham Lincoln.

Let us — you and I — search through the story of this sad-faced, stoop-shouldered giant among men. We shan't spend very much time retelling the story of his life. There is little already untold. From the vigorous labors of his boyhood, the loves and the ruggedness of his young manhood, the education which he gained — through the only method by which one may ever in the world gain an education — by disciplining his own mind and manners, and by collecting his own facts, and by sorting them and associating them *himself* for the kind of uses his *own* mind may need to put them to. You know about these things already, just as you know the majestic beauty of that raw-boned kindly face before which generations of boys and girls have paused and sighed in awe and walked on bigger and better and broader and more kind. All that picture is plain to every American. And it stands out sharply in all of our minds like the gleaming statue itself.

But today, search with me among the shadows *behind* Lincoln. It's an adventure more Americans of today and of tomorrow need.

How in the world did such a man as Abraham Lincoln ever happen to be elected to the Presidency of the United States? It was an accident! In the East, men were learning to harness the machine into great factories. And they were collecting and crowding men into cities around those factories. Great webs of railraods were reaching out farther and farther into the West, bringing with them the capitalist and the sharper. The morality, decency and the honor in businessmen, which had once been an important part in success, was now fast becoming greased and grimey from the stationary machine in the factory and the rolling one on the steel rails. These rails brought men, driven from the Eastern factories by the incoming shiploads of cheap foreign workers, out into the West. But the long tentacles of the railroads reached out after them and ruined their lives and their fortunes with unjust tolls and impossible debts.

The West hated the East with its merciless financiers who drove old men and women and growing boys and girls, to slave beside the others in their filthy unventilated factories in order to keep from actually starving.

And then, there was the South with its agriculture and its slaves. The industrial city Northerners despised the Southern slave-holding farmers. And the Southerners hated and distrusted the Northerners. From the platforms of Boston self-righteous men shouted, "These cruel wretches of the South take away from the poor helpless colored race his freedom, and drive him like a domesticated beast!" And from the platforms of Savannah, the Southerner shouted, "We pay from $1,500 to $2,500 for our slave. We feed him well. We clothe him. And we care for him in sickness or in health, so that he may live long and work well, and we can get our money's worth out of him. But what of the factory slaves of Philadelphia and Boston and New York? — Underfed, ill-housed, ill-clothed, over-worked into worthlessness and sickness, and then thrown out! The men of the North are villains!" Then came the time for the Convention of the Republicans in Chicago to nominate their Presidential candidate. The delegates of hte East had gone to Chicago as a matter of form to nominate the capitalist governor of New York— Seward. "It was in the bag!" Bu tth emen of the West were angry They crashed the gates of the Conveniton. And the poor stunned delegates from the East suddenly awoke to find themselves with the gaunt, coarse, unpolished, uneducated, backwoodsman on their hands — for Presidential timber! Even his voice was thin and tight and weak.

New York and Boston and all the points East gasped in horror. And when, in the elections, the voice of the common people — the common people of the West and the pitiable laborers from the East — decided that this man was to be the next President, the humiliation of the great leaders knew no bounds.

Within a few weeks the South withdrew itself from the United States of America, and said that they would set up their own government. The rotten timbers and the broken planks of the floundering Ship of State had finally pulled apart. And the wreck lay helplessly awash in the seas running high with jealousy and hatred and dishonesty and self-righteousness. At the trembling wheel stood, almost alone, this tall sad-faced Westerner who had taken his sacred oath on an old Book — one of the three from which he had gotten most of his education. He had promised, before God, that he would uphold the Constitution of the United States of America to the best of his ability. And to him that promise meant exactly that.

For himself he hated the idea of slavery. But as the President of the United States whose Constitution permitted slavery, he was not interested except as slavery endangered the unity of the nation.

Then, and not until then, did he finally come to the conclusion that slavery must die in order that the Union might live. Not until then did he proclaim that the slaves should be freed.

Long before the firing upon Fort Sumter sounded the actual beginning of the struggle of brother against brother, the conflagration of hatred had been lighted and its vicious, unintelligent flame was being fanned by the prattle of such second-rate poets as James Russell Lowell, and by such passion-lashing exaggerations as Harriet Beecher Stowe's "Uncle Tom's Cabin," and her "Life in the Dismal Swamp."

Out from this background of the din and the stench of human misery and blundering and meanness — the profiteering traitor, the sneaking orator, the beastly murderous passions of hatred and blindness — out of the black filth of this background stood that humble heavy-hearted man, who had risen from the lowly deep heart of Democracy — honest and clean — a man who could utter the calm simple sincere words of his undying Gettysburg address (and every American should know it as the Democratic alphabet). While the flames of hatred and selfishness and of dismal fear were lapping up even unto his very face — a man whose noble soul could speak clearly in the midst of his countryman's struggle — could say, "With malice toward none, with charity for all, with firmness in the right as God gives us to see the right, let us strive on to finisn the work we are in — to bind up the Nation's wounds — to do all which may achieve and cherish a *just* and lasting peace among ourselves and with all nations."

And then, the war was won! He was the victor, ready to deal with the prostrate vanquished. When someone suggested that Jefferson Davis should be hung, as the much loved "Gloria Hallelujah" song suggested, the President — in *fact* again — of the *United* States, smiled, "Judge not that *ye* be not judged" — and again — "There is too much desire on the part of some of our very good friends to be masters — to interfere and to dictate to those states — to treat the people not as fellow citizens. There is too little respect for their rights. I do not sympathize with these feelings."

And then the greatest tragedy which our Nation had ever known! Abraham Lincoln was murdered! — — —

So spoke the Captain with the mighty heart. And when the judgment thunders split the house, wrenching the rafters from their ancient rest, he held the ridgepole up and spiked again the rafters of the Home. He held his place — held on through blame and faltered not at praise. And when he fell in whirlwind, he went down as when a lordly cedar, green with boughs, goes down with a great shout upon the hill, and leaves a lonesome place against the sky.

It was not his death that so much mattered, nor the manner of it. Death must come to us all. The war had been won. The Union was preserved. But love and honesty and brotherly kindness and peace took flight with the soul of Abraham Lincoln.

The story of what followed his death as America waded back toward civilization — the story is so unhappy that we seldom tell it, and never write it into our history books. In all the history of modern civilized nations, there is no parallel for that situation which existed in our own country! It is almost unbelieveable! No civilized victor has ever been more ungenerous. But through it all — shining out through the darkness and the misery — was the light of the soul of Abraham Lincoln, who died believing in the *goodness* of men.

MEMORIAL DAY

This day never seemed to me to be a great time for a wild and happy celebration, nor on the other hand, for droll, and dry, and tearful oratorical wailing. I'm sure that the lad who has come to the time when his tired hand slowly relaxed its grip on the rifle, and he lay down for his long rest in peace at last — I'm sure that lad would wish least of all that the still free folks he loved back home — that they should suffer and mourn for him on such a lovely day as this. I'm sure he'd be tickled to see them go'ng fishing — with the family all together. He'd smile to know how they will be thrilled here in a little while as they watch the races down in Indianapolis, and I'm also sure he'd be personally proud to watch his Dad back home on the farm refusing to take the day off when the corn or the soybeans or the other chores needed to be tended, or the fences fixed, or whatever job needed to be done. For long before that lad found peace he had learned to face death — as the natural and inevitable thing that it is. And even though he probably resented the good fun he'd be missing out on if his number came up, still . . . "Well, it's just one of those things" . . . he would have said "Somebody's got to do it."

Somebody's got to do it! And some of us still have to do it, friends; it surely hasn't been done. These lads of ours, these sons and daughters, these brave young lovers and husbands, this proud young daddy who may never have seen that kid of his, this youngster who didn't get to have the feel of his challenging new career before the call to sacrifice came — these lads of ours were struggling to do the job of bringing peace to the folks back home, and to save the world. But all they succeeded in doing was to find peace for *themselves*.

Somebody still has to do it. Somebody has to find the road to *peace*, and *security*, and *freedom*, and *justice* for the common folks in this world. Somebody has to find the real cause of this horrible human disease . . . War . . . which has never, and never will, bring any good to the world; only pain and sin and debauchery and death and confusion. Yes, and less and less of *freedom*. Someone must find the real cause and strike at that cause. Until then, these dead shall have died in vain, and more must still die.

Profits and politics; investigations and inventions; oratory and organizations; more oratory and more committees; more armaments and mobilization; more oratory and more committees; — these things may ease the pain but they'll never cure the disease

— the disease of hatred and war and misunderstanding. Wherever they sleep — these lads of ours and of our enemies — wherever they sleep within their tents of green that dot the world, they know that peace can come only in the souls of men who have minds that can understand and are willing to pay the real price of *Peace* and *Freedom*. And that is to permit other men to live at peace, and to be free.

It's an individual and lonely thing — dying. Even among the thousands of his fighting comrades, a boy is all alone with death, except for that gentle voice which says, "Come with me." And for those of us who pledge so blithely that "we here highly resolve that these dead shall not have died in vain" as is carved in an impressive scroll across the gleaming marble arch behind the tomb of our Unknown Soldier, to us who make that pledge, living is also an all alone thing.

We keep the pledge "all alone," each man of us, each woman, each boy or girl — all alone. And no one but ourself knows whether we are fulfilling that pledge to see to it that these lads shall not have died in vain — alone. Today each one of us stands *alone* in that mighty bivouac camp of green. And eyes made wise by having looked at last upon peace and truth, are asking us each one, "What have *you* done to see to it that we have *not* died in vain?" And each of us must answer, *alone* — must answer, "This much I have done. This much I have failed to do."

(Awarded FREEDOM'S FOUNDATION Honor Certificate, February, 1966)

CHRISTMAS

Year after year — and I don't know how many of those years — I have talked to you along about this time about Christmas and its meaning, about Peace on Earth, about the teachings of the one whose birthday we are celebrating — so many of us — in such a shallow and thoughtless way. But this morning I'd like to talk sort of straight from me to you. I am sick and tired of the far away "somebody else" lessons that we are always having preached over us around Christmas time. Let us see, for a change, what we may find in the philosophy of the great Teacher whose birthday has become the greatest holiday in the world. Let us see what we may find in His philosophy of Peace on the Earth, Good Will Toward Men, which directly concerns us — here — now — today. And by "us" I mean you and me and not they and them.

When Jesus was born in Bethlehem of Judea in the days of Herod the King, angels sang that here was one who was to bring Peace on the Earth and Good Will Toward Men. They were badly mistaken. There has been no peace on the earth and very little good will among men. In fact, because of the teachings and philosophies of Jesus, many of our most cruel and brainless and useless wars have been perpetrated upon the human race. You must admit along with me that this is true.

And then He started His magnificent attempt to deliver His message of love and good will to the sons of Man. I see Him touching with His hands the loathome, horrible outcasts — the lepers. I see Him calmly smiling with understanding at the blustering cowardly Peter who had been be-deviled into denying his faith three times in a single night. I see Him standing in the crowd as the village gossips presented the woman whom they had taken in adultery. The people mill around Him waiting for His words of reproach to this wretch whose sin — in those days — was an unspeakable one. He looks into the eyes of His audience — "Go get stones," He commands. They hurry away — surely she should be stoned to death — the shameful woman! She is kneeling — hopeless. They are ready — the rocks poised over their heads, ready to bruise the life from the sin-drenched body before them. I see Him hold up His hand. All is silent. "Let him who is guiltless among you —," He looks straight into their eyes. "Let him who is guiltless among you cast the *first* stone." But no one threw — any more than you would have thrown, or I.

I see Him dining with those disciples of His who were nearest to His heart and in whose hands rested the sowing of the seed of

His thoughts and ideals. They are quarreling among themselves as to who is to be the most highly honored in the Kingdom of Heaven. I see Him smile whimsically. "He who is greatest among you," He says, "let him be servant of all."

I see Him weeping alone in the shadows of His last night. The others sleep. They are tired — He would not waken them. I see Him accepting with dignity and understanding the humiliating death which His society dealt to dangerous radicals. He *was* a radical. We would have done the same. We do the same here now — today.

I see Him suspended between heaven and earth. In the swift inventory of His futile attempt to change the hearts and the minds of men, perhaps He looked ahead for two thousand years into my heart and your heart. Do we wonder that He cried, "My God, My God, why hast Thou forsaken me?"

From that hour until today, you and I, like Judas, have betrayed the good and the right and the true for thirty pieces of silver. You and I, like Peter, have denied the sweet and the clean and the beautiful for the sake of soul-murdering conformity — for the sake of being accepted as "one of them" by groups who have sacrificed their own thoughts, their own brains, their own beliefs, to the thinking and the ritual of the Organization. You, and I, too, have ripped to pieces the great truths of life as the people did His raiment. And have been satisfied with half-truths that we clutch to our poisoned minds because we were too lazy and afraid to search further until we found the whole truth. You, and I, too, have plaited a crown of thorns and have crushed it down upon the bleeding brows of the honest and the wise, who are great enought to try to show us our evils — who were great enough to try to search for the whole truths — who were great enough to stand alone. And each day, you and I again crucify His message — that we love one another.

Well, what is this love for our fellow man which He aspired to give to us? It isn't what I used to think it was. I don't feel like running up to anyone here and throwing my arms around them. In fact, as I figure this thing out, this love is not really an emotion it is far superior to an emotion. It is purely intellectual — the product of clear, careful thought. I'm going to call it understanding, and to understand means to have thought and reasoned and observed until one sees clearly.

I don't know if I can explain to you what I am driving at, but let us take some examples: I know you. You are light-fingered. You can not be trusted. You steal. If the law gets you, you will be put in jail good and promptly, for our property is the one thing which we Americans still hold sacred. Your neighbors talk about you and shun you and despise you. You are crooked. You're a thief. But I do not hate you. I, too, have stolen things. I have taken things that I didn't earn, and that didn't belong to me, including minutes from other people's lives and that's what life is when you think of it — just minutes added together. But again, I don't hate you, thief. Somewhere in your inheritance or in your rearing something has been left out. Perhaps it is the demand in your own character that you must earn it and deserve it before you can have it. It isn't your fault. I understand — I like you. Come to my home — be my friend.

You have loose morals. People say unspeakable things about your behavior. One who cares for the respect of society must keep away from you. It's too bad! Somewhere in your make-up a lack of balance has been made between your mind and your desires. Maybe when you were a little fellow and the patterns of your life were being formed, you let yourself get away with making a hog of yourself eating candy or cookies or dessert. Maybe you were not trained way back then to obey the orders of the better part of your brain — you didn't learn *self*-discipline. Well, I have a sister and a mother and a little girl who are sweet too. Come be my friend. Perhaps we may find some interesting work in which your desires may learn discipline or be forgotten.

You are a mean man to do business with. People hate you for your unscrupulous dealings. You're crooked. That's too bad! Here in America money is our God, and you should know his throne must be approached according to a certain ritual. If it is, we call it good business. If not, then you are a shyster. But come with me. We shall study the methods. Mayhap we shall be able to make a million dollars — which no living man could ever *earn*. We must learn to deal in business according to the ritual. But seriously, maybe you can learn the satisfaction of dealing on the square — of *earning* the profits that you want for the enrichment of your life.

You are a good-for-nothing, lazy nincompoop. On the job you are undependable and uninterested. The "goof-off" is a part of your approach to your employment. Ah, the tragedy of it! From your life has been taken one of its greatest joys. The joy of work. Come with me. Be my friend. It isn't too late to recapture one of life's greatest satisfactions, and that's work well done.

You are a murderer. In fact, you have broken all of the Ten Commandments. But the One whose birthday we celebrate today gave another one and it was this: He said, "But a greater commandment than these I give unto you." And He was speaking of all of the Ten — "But a greater commandment than these I give unto you — that you love one another." Come be my friend. Be the friend of another criminal and perhaps together we can find a new road — a road so very few have ever taken.

Maybe I failed to make myself clear in this little preachment as I invite other sinners, like me, to be my guests — to be my friends. But perhaps, that way we could learn to worship God together. The great Teacher whose birthday we celebrate said, "How can you love God whom you have not seen unless you love your brother whom you have seen?" At least, may I suggest this to you as a Christmas adventure?

WHY CHRISTMAS THE 25th OF DECEMBER

A Christmas Eve Story

I don't know if I'll be able to pass along to you what for many years has been a genuine adventure in thinking to me, but I should like to try it if I may. Hundreds of years before the birth of Jesus, December 25th had been one of the world's greatest holidays. The date was actually wrong because of a mistake made by the early star gazers, who had figured December 25th to be the date of the winter solstice. You see, to all of us who live north of the equator, this is about the time of the year when the days are the shortest and the nights are the longest, and so we call it the first of winter.

However, the early star gazers, as I told you, had made a slight mistake and thought that this winter solstice, or the change from fall to winter, came on the 25th instead of on the 21st or 22nd, as it actually does. That is the date when the earth has tilted to the farthest point away from the sun, and from that date, the days begin to get a little longer, and the nights a little shorter. So all through the ages before Jesus, those who lived north of the equator celebrated that day as the beginning of the slow journey of the sun as it seemed to travel back from the south, and travel higher and higher in the southern sky. Long before Jesus' time, the pagans had celebrated the 25th of December, as the feast of the birth of the new sun. The Egyptians celebrated the 25th as the day when their sun goddess, Isis, made her welcome return from the south. The ancient Gauls and the Bretons began their 12-day pagan festival to the returning sun on that day. The Germans welcomed the return of their sun wheel and watched closely for the 12 days following to see what their deities Odin and Berchta would do during the year. The yule log, the holly, the mistletoe, the wassail bowl — are all relics of these ancient celebrations of the winter solstice and the beginning of the lengthening day.

And then came Christianity. It probably is good for us to recall that the Christian religion was born, without question, among the poor and the unlettered and the simple peoples of the world. And it was before that friendly, humble, soft-spoken Nazarene had begun His teaching that there was a kind and loving Heavenly Father and that all the high and the low, the rich and the poor, the simple and the wise, were His beloved children with their birthright of dignity and of freedom. It was long before His time that December 25th had been the greatest of the world's holidays. Then came Christianity. And with the same striking simplicity and the high respect for the law and for the decent customs of the people, there was no attempt at all by the early Christians to create new festival days. For you see, it is never the poor and the humble — the laborer — the common folks — who finally decide which day shall be a holiday, but always the employer, the government, the powerful. And so, since Easter had been held as a holy day by the Jews — the day on which they celebrated their Feast of the Passover and their deliverance from the yoke of Egyptian bondage, and since in Babylon Easter day had long been held in honor of the legendary god, Ishtar, and in Greece, had been a day of wild pagan revel in commemoration of the resurrection of Adonis, so it too became the day set aside by the Christians to recall the resurrection of *their* Lord. Likewise, December 25th, the greatest of all *pagan* holidays, was set by the early believers in lives of gentle kindness and love — the followers of the quiet Nazarene — for their kind of feast day, to remember the day of His birth (because no one had any idea at all of when Jesus was born).

And slowly throughout all the world, as people began to be converted to the Christian religion, and the pagan severity of the ancient holiday was softened and sweetened by this new religion, Christmas became the gentle holiday of love that it is today. Of course, in the meantime there was a long black period when the Christian church became the most wealthy and the most powerful, yes — and I guess you can say — the most brutal organization that the world had ever seen. But that is a story which might better be told on some other evening than on Christmas Eve.

• • •

However, it is a wonderful adventure to follow the story of what happened through the ages to the teachings of that clear-eyed lover of all men who came to bring peace on the poor earth — through the welter of the heathenish bloody crusades, and then through the revolt in which a large number of thoughtful men, and also thoughtless men, tried to bring back the self-denial and the simplicity and the democracy of the beginnings. And how, out of that revolt sprang thousands of sects of Christianity, quarreling, and hating and killing, until the rigorous war-like hating Puritans had destroyed almost all forms of art and of tolerance and of freedom. It's a long adventure story full of many unpleasant chapters, the story that was begun in a manger in Bethlehem of Judea. But for this Christmas Eve, let's forget those chapters and think of an amazing story, one that is difficult for us to understand. For, after all, you must remember with what shock the American people themselves felt, and what a furor resulted when Franklin Delano Roosevelt changed our Thanksgiving Day — the President of the United States changed it! And then you look back and realize that here was the poorest and the humblest and the simplest of the folks who succeeded in bringing about an almost complete metamorphosis of the greatest of the year's holidays in their lands. You can see perhaps something of the incomprehensible power of that gentle Nazarene who shocked the world by saying to the proud religionists, "For as much as ye have done it unto the least of these my brothers, ye have done it unto me" — the least of these.

Here was the tap root of all the best that there is in Democracy today. Here was that message which has been nearly lost in every generation since the story was begun in the manger in Bethlehem of Judea — His teachings, that every man and every woman has a right to a share in the kingdom of heaven, that each body is a temple of the living God, that it is the pure in heart the peace-maker, the poor, the merciful, who is truly blessed. And even today, with His dream unfulfilled, we still hope and pray that there may come future chapters in this story when peace on earth and good will among men shall surely be.

But once again, as we think of Christmas time as the time when the sun has gone as far away from us as it will in the year, it might be a good time to hope that longer days of *real* light in our thinking and the increasing warmth that comes from the light of truth that He gave us, may bring us back to the renewal of growth and hope that comes with spring, and when the warmth and the light of His teachings comes back to bring Peace on Earth, and Good Will to men.

THE GREATEST THOUGHT

"Peace on the earth," the angels sang
To shepherds in the night:
A star gleamed over Bethlehem.
The shepherds shook with fright.

The manger where the baby lay
Beneath His mother's eyes,
Became the center of the world
Of simple men, and wise.

And, when He grew to be a man,
Thoughtful and strong and tall,
He offered to the world a thought —
A simple thought was all.

But selfish men and foolish men,
Distorting what He said,
Built temples, killed, and prayed, and fought,
And sought for power instead.

'Twas such a simple thought He gave
To just be left behind —
"Love one another." That was all.
But it would save mankind.

AS FROM THE DARKNESS

As from the darkness, in the east the star
Shone on the wise men, lighting up their way —
Leading their weary feet to hallowed inn —
To lowly manger where the baby lay;
And as the angels sang, "Behold we bring
"Good tidings: Peace on earth, good will toward men.",
And bade the trembling shepherds fear no more,
And hills and valleys echoed back, "Amen" . . .
So shines today the star's immortal beam
On humble lowly hearts, as it did then,
And STILL the angels sing — if we could hear —
"Peace on the earth, and good will t'ward all men."
And men, grown weary with the striving world,
STILL pause in streets or in the fields of corn
And from their hearts, join in the angels' song
With: "Hallelujah, for a Christ is born!"

BABE OF BETHLEHEM

To you, little babe, lying snug and fragrant in the manger of Bethlehem
   I cannot afford to bring gifts of gold and frankincense and myrrh.
No unusual voices have spoken to me from the heavens to announce that
   A Savior is born who shall bring peace on the earth and good will among men.

No star has shined in the East to show me which way to go.
   But you'll understand, I think — Babe of Bethlehem.
Because your folks are poor folks too . . . You'll understand when
   I offer you this —
                    My gift: —

I'll try to be worthy of the stewardship of my soil
   From which the bodies and minds and souls of my fellowmen grow.
Each day I shall try to help men to hear the voice of your Father
   As He speaks to them from the deep spaces between the stars,
From the patter of raindrops in the summer shower,
   From the beaming warm bosom of the living soil,
And from the miracle of the lowly blade of grass.

And, Holy Babe of Bethlehem, there are so many other babies in the world!
   And you love them too — each one of them.
And each one is the hope of the world too, and the beloved son of your Father.

I may never see you. But you'll understand if I do to them —
   To the boys and girls — what I would do to you
If you were one of the neighbor's kids — just growing up.

I can't afford gifts of gold and frankincense and myrrh.
   But I can give you a loyal heart and all that I am
To help bring peace on the earth and good will among men.

CHRISTMAS GREETING

You've hitched your horses to the sleigh,
Their bells and harness jingling.
Cozy on oat straw . . . blanket-wrapped,
Your nose and ears are tingling.
  The lane is banked with drifted snow,
  With sparkling diamonds studded.
  And fence-row bushes, ermine-decked,
  With icy pearls are budded.
    Sleigh whispers softly through the snow.
    Clouds from your team's breath rises
    And floats above your fur-capped heads.
    Each road-turn brings surprises.
      A cardinal in scarlet dress
      Across the wood comes riding.
      A rabbit track across the field
      Gives hint of where he's hiding.
        Over the bridge and down the hill
        You and your folks come singing.
        And I and my folks   here at home,
        Wait for the joy you're bringing.
You're here at last! You all pile out,
With hand-clasps, hugs, and kisses.
We're all together once again!!
A Merry Christmas this is!!
  Your team out to the fragrant barn,
  Unbridled . . . bedded deep,
  And blanketed to keep them warm.
  The cattle and the sheep
    Call out. The rooster crows his song.
    Old Pepper barks with glee,
    Escorting us up to the house —
    Together — YOU and ME!
      The cozy kitchen welcomes us
      With Christmas Dinner dream —
      Aroma of the cooking things,
      Wood smoke, teakettle's steam.
        The parlor Round Oak . . . belly-red,
        Gleaming in warming cheer,
        The center of our circle stands.
        How GLAD we are YOU'RE here!!
A dream, I know, is all it is.
We *will* be far apart.

But Christmas we *will* meet like this —
Together in my heart.
   For at our house, you see, you share
   Our Christmas just the same.
   And when it's night we all will be
   So thankful that you came.
      A Merry Christmas to you all,
      From Belle Lea Acres! Hear?
      And may your best dreams all come true
      Throughout a grand New Year!

CHRISTMAS GREETING

Miserly I crouch, with Christmas near,
And peer within the wallet of my heart
At the dear soul-gems I have hoarded there.
Each is special. There are but a few.
But they make Life of life . . .
And one . . . is you.

CHRISTMAS GREETING

The calm of snow;
The cheer of icy winds;
The stately wisdom of undaunted trees,
Standing aloof mid Winter's bitterness;
The cruel friendliness of lapping flame . . .
(I bathe in sunshine from his victim's heart.)

The noisy solitude of Christmas cheer;
The feast; the laughter; the thin greetings gay;
The rush; the revels; and the loud farewells;
The gifts, so dearly bought, hastily given;
These, from my heart, wring cries of loneliness.
Grant me, I beg you, this one Christmas gift:
Think of our love today . . . for just an hour.

CHRISTMAS GREETING

Dust of the road is on the shrubs and grass;
Mud that has spattered from the cars that pass;
Leaves that a month ago were bright and gay
Are sodden now in colorless decay.
Drab, dull, and lifeless are the fields and wood,
And ragged spectres where the roses stood.

Then comes the snow! And through the silent night
Blankets my whole world with its perfect white.
A gleaming new and living world it brings
With children's laughter . . . and the old heart sings . . .
The miracle of snow that hides the old
And warms the spirit with its very cold.

●   ●   ●

Dust of the year is on my heart and mind;
Mud that has spattered from the thoughts unkind;
Hopes, that a month ago were bright and gay,
Are sodden now in colorless decay.
Drab, dull, and lifeless lie the days ahead.
As ragged spectres stand my dreams, long dead.

And then comes Christmas, stealing softly in
All imperceptible, amid the din
Of rushing labor and of tired play;
And suddenly . . . I am another Jay.
My world is blanketed with hope and cheer;
My doubts and worries strangely disappear;

My old heart revels in warm thoughts of friends;
And all the challenge that a new day sends.
These Christmas miracles each year renew
My faith, my hope, my joy in friends like you,
And life again is good, and hope is dear.
You have helped make it so, again this year.

CHRISTMAS GREETING

Christmas Spirit hit Fort Wayne quite early again.
In fact, at the merchants' fall meeting
'Twas agreed that we'd make it a record this year
That no other town would be beating.

So on lamp-posts and buildings all over the town
We hung up the new decorations
That cried "Merry Christmas" all Thanksgiving Day.
And the TV and radio stations

Began playing Christmas songs right through the day
From Friday, the twenty-eighth morning.
And we all joined in singing the old Christmas song,
With the "get your gifts mailed early" warning.

Between "Silent Night" and "Cantique de Noel"
We sold soap and perfume and beer.
And among the hog-wormers and candy and paint
We interspersed good Christmas cheer.

Some call it "commercialization" and cry,
"Why not bring Christ back into Christmas?"
Well to me, He seems more of a part every year
Of the holiday — Arctic to Isthmus.

Sure there's selling. That's bad? And there's buying. That's
good?
Spending's more fun than saving's my story.
And the Church doings do pretty well for themselves
Clear from fish-fries up to offertory.

Giving presents is fun. So is getting them, too.
That's a part of the Christmas tradition.
There are sobering moments for me, I confess,
When I ponder my purse's condition.

Like today now . . . It's flat. But poodaddle! So what?
Would Jay let such a little thing throw him?
I just take up my pencil, and set myself down,
And write you a new Christmas poem.

And with it, I send along, good friend of mine,
A heart-full of friendship to you
And a big Merry Christmas and Happy New Year
And my Thanks for the good things you do.

CHRISTMAS GREETING

The bells ring loud and the bells ring long,
And the bells ring sharp and cold;
The horns and the drums and the singing strings
With their voices soft or bold . . .
The girls sing high and the boys sing low . . .
And they all blend in to cheer
With a song or a rhyme for the year's best time,
For the "Christmas Spirit's" here!

The pine and the holly and the gew-gaws jolly
Set the stage for the Christmas fun.
The Christmas-present buying, with just everybody trying
For the right gift for everyone . . .
The pretty card that others send their friends and aunts and
    mothers
With the pictures and the greetings gay —
All combine to make the splendor that the season does engender
Of the greatest holiday.

· · ·

The hucksters cry, "Come buy! Come buy!
"At Christmas bargain prices."
Store windows gleam like a child-hood dream
With a thousand sales devices.
"You don't need cash for your buying rash.
"Use your credit card or borrow!
"Live it up! Show you're rich! Sing it high! Keep the pitch!
"You can always pay tomorrow.
"The Christmas swing is the only thing . . .
"You can be the life of the party!
"Laugh loud! Talk fast! Dance hard! Leave last!
"Drink 'Christmas cheer'! Be hearty!"

· · ·

Now the crowd is gone. And it's almost dawn.
Through the darkness I walk alone.
I raise my eye to the Christmas sky.
The wind has a sombre tone . . .

And soft through the night in a lone star's light
Comes a gentle Voice and clear:
"I brought you love. I brought you peace.
"I brought you surcease from fear.
"I pointed the way of gentleness,
"To live with one another —
"To help you see what the world would be
"With each man each man's brother."

But my own heart cries as the sweet voice dies
And I gaze at the lonely star;
"We have lost our way! What is there to say?
"We have missed it, oh so far!"

Oh, the bells ring loud and the bells ring long
From the steeples or the towers.
But they ring in vain to the Christmas strain
Till HIS peace and HIS love are ours.

A SMILE

A smile is the warmest sunshine
That shines at any pole.
But the smile that stays the longest is
The smile that comes from the soul.

That smile that's more than stretching your face
And showing all your teeth —
That genuine smile that reflects the glow
Of a happy heart underneath.

It's good to smile when you're happy.
It's an easy thing to do.
But I think it's better and braver to smile
When you're really sad, don't you?

And so often Life demands that you smile,
For you have to play a part.
And the show must go on with a smile and a song,
No matter how heavy your heart.

And, I think, it's the wise and the manly thing
And the womanly thing to do,
To stick out your chin whatever the day
May bring, and smile, don't you?

(Recitation to accompany "Smiles")

Through the years, we have used recitations to add a little more meaning to some of the songs, The stanzas to follow are a few of them:

THE CALL OF GOD

The call of God is to many tasks —
To many tasks, my son.
And the final victory depends
On how your task is done.

Not on the glory of the day —
The volume of the praise,
Nor can you judge of your success
By how much gold it pays.

The call of God is to the plow —
To till for Him the soil,
To fill the day from dawn to dark
With silent humble toil.

The call is to the market place,
Upon the busy street,
To rolling sea, to timbered hill,
To servant's tired feet.

For some, the call to namelessness;
For some, the call to fame . . .
To shovel or to sceptre,
All are to God the same.

But this will never change, my son.
This will be always true:
Success in life is doing well
What God would have you do.

(Recitation to accompany hymn, "I'll Go Where You Want Me To Go")

THE AGE OF TRUTH

I guess it never seemed to me as holy as it should.
I guess I wasn't born to be so very very good.
'Twas almost more than I could bear to sit so still so long
And wait until the minister announced the closing song.

And mother always looked so sad, and father oh, so stern!
Until the benediction came, it was a sin to turn
And look at Mrs. Beebe's hat and Uncle Elmer's head —
Smooth as an apple on the top, and more than half as red.

Yet in that little village church there seemed to come a spell;
A peace, a calm serenity, a feeling all was well
With everything in all the world, and everything was good.
And in my childish heart I felt a kind of brotherhood.

And every living thing I loved. And everything was fair.
I don't know what to call the spell. Perhaps it was a prayer.
And sometimes yet I feel it . . . now that I've gone away.
And when it comes I always wish that I could make it stay —

That little church's miracle I love so to recall —
A simple childish faith that things are all right after all.

(Recitation to accompany song, "Voice in the Old Village Choir")

HOME AGAIN

I left that scrubby little shack ten years ago to-day.
Oh, I was glad to leave that dump, and go for miles away.
I used to walk for blocks around and sneak back there alone
To keep my friends from knowing that I lived in such a home.

And mother's dresses were so old and patched and out-of-date!
I had to look the other way when she stood at the gate.
And when she'd call "Hello" to me, her voice was shrill and thin;
Not soft and smooth, like others were in places I had been.

So I left home and went to live where no one knew my shame.
And I professed a home of wealth ... I even changed my name ...
That was ten years ago to-day. But, since then, I have seen
Enough of life to recognize the things that make a queen.

I'm going home where love is pure, and where someone is true!
I'm going home to shanty-town ... and going to stay there, too.
For silks and furs and gems and gold and the affected grace
Of bright-light butterflies can never match my mother's face.

(Recitation to accompany song, "Shanty in Old Shanty-Town")

LADY MAKE-BELIEVE

You naughty, naughty daddy's girl,
You've stolen up the stair
And opened Mummy's old, old trunk
With all her yesterwear!

You've gowned yourself in style all right —
That hat's hind-side before!
That lacy gown you're wearing there
A-trailing on the floor —

Is one your Mummy wore that night —
I see her now so plain —
So sweet and lovely and so proud,
And so unused to pain.

Those tall laced boots, with heels so high,
Scarce touched the floor at all
When, like a bird, your Mummy floated,
Waltzing 'round the hall.

That muff in which your paddies hide . . .
You'd never guess . . . It's true . . .
My own hand found your Mummy's there,
And that was how I knew.

Be careful how you step, Madam —
With that long tangled gown!
And wobbling shoes . . . Ooops . . . there you go!
I thought they'd get you down!

There! Now you're up as good as new!
A lovely lady . . . see?
Your hand, Madame; I'd be so proud
If you would waltz with me!

● ● ●

You lovely little make-believe
A-waltzing with your dad!
Who'd ever guess this gown would see
The gaiety it's had?

Dream, Little Lady Make-Believe!
And, may there someday be
Someone to bring you half the joy
That you have brought to me.

(Recitation to accompany song, "Lady Make-Believe")

OLD FASHIONED ROSES

I am in the same old garden that we planted — you and I —
In those happy, happy days when you were here.
And, on the fence the morning-glories nod at passers-by;
And those humble homely holly-hocks this year
Have grown up so thick and tall, they almost hide the seat we made
On that Sunday afternoon. Do you recall?
When I planted that old fashioned bush of roses in the shade,
And you laughed and said they'd never bloom at all.

I am standing in the garden, and I still can see you there
On your knees where the Narcissus grew.
And the sun is still caressing the soft wisps of wayward hair;
And the roses bending over you.
They are blooming now, and lovely — the old fashioned roses are.
See? I'll pick a lovely bouquet just for you.
And I'll hold it toward the sunset, for I know you can't be far.
I am sure the garden feels your presence too.

See? They're lovely, don't you think so? I have tended them
  each day.
You can see them, can't you, dear, from where you are?
Seems to me they've grown more fragrant, darling, since you
  went away —
But I'm sure you haven't gone so very far . . .
For the sky is close above me, and the sunset just beyond
Where the silver maple stands a-top the hill.
I can almost see you smiling, for you always were so fond
Of those dear old fashioned roses. Are you still?

(Recitation to accompany song, "A Garland of Old Fashioned Roses")

THIS MUSIC BUSINESS

This music is a funny thing —
A funny thing, you know!
It's just too deep to figure out,
For everywhere you go

And everything you do all day
Is followed by a song.
And, if it weren't so, the days
Would all be twice as long.

And, though we do about the same
Old things the ages through —
And, though the trees and flowers and sky
And love are nothing new —

Each day a brand new song is born —
A brand new melody —
To sing the very same old things:
The love, the life, the play.

You'd think the spring of human song
Would finally run dry —
And no new melodies be found
About love and the sky!

You'd think the song of young love's dream,
Of "yes" beneath the moon,
Of Springtime and of mother
Would be all exhausted soon!

It's one of Nature's miracles —
Each day all things are new —
Faces and babies . . . stars and love . . .
And songs and souls and you . . .

No two alike . . . Forever new!
And then to each belong —
Never repeated . . . never old . . .
Life's miracle — a song.

(Recitation to accompany original song, "I Have a Song")

THESE LOVE SONGS!

I just can't seem to understand,
The only thing they sing
About, is Love — day in, day out —
Love and no other thing!

An apple tree — they sing of Love.
They see an old mill stream,
And so they sing a song of love.
It's love for coffee cream!

Sunshine and Love . . . And sunset, too . . .
And sleet and snow and rain!
At harvest time they stop to love.
Well, what about the grain?

Why, every time the moon comes out
The songs would make it seem
The boys hang 'round like hound dogs,
And howl and bay and scream!

Don't anybody love the sun
And flowers and stars above,
And work and play and sleep and dreams
Unless they're sick on LOVE?

(Recitation to accompany original song, "Fooey on Love")

FADED OLD LOVE LETTERS

A pile of mildewed pages
  In this discarded chest;
A heap of smould'ring mem'ries
  I find here in my breast.

I feel those soft warm fingers
  I once held in my hand . . .
Hearts and the moon were mellow
  That night upon the sand!

And, at the hour of parting
  We swore beneath the sky
That our love would be true indeed,
  Until we both should die.

How I recall the mellow moon!
  How I re-feel the bliss!
And, how warm yet the sacrament
  Of that heart-sealing kiss!

And then Fate tore us far apart,
  But letters came each day,
Until, at last, a letter came
  To say, "She's gone away."

The years with slow and tired step
  Have passed . . . But none too soon . . .
For all my heart was sealed to love
  Beneath that mellow moon.

•   •   •

A pile of mildewed pages
  In this discarded chest;
A heap of smould'ring mem'ries
  Within an empty breast.

(Recitation to accompany song, "Those Faded Old Love Letters")

LITTLE OLD LADY

Come, little old lady — come walk with me.
Come walk in the land that used to be.
Put on your little old bonnet and shawl,
And forget your troubles, your age and all.
And dream of the days that you used to know,
When you were a belle with your handsome beau.

Yes, then in the evening your laughter rang.
Just kids like us — you also sang
And played and danced the night away
Till the woodland echoed your voices gay.
And, little old lady, do you recall
The polka you danced at the village ball?

Then, little old lady, you, too, stayed long
At the garden gate, when the party was done.
And you said "good night," again and again
Instead of once, as it should have been.
Ah, little old lady, your eyes are bright
As you dream again of that "good night!"

Come, Little Old Lady, your dream is done.
But wasn't it truly a little fun
To go back with us boys and us girls to the day
When you, too were foolish and young and gay?
Come, Little Old Lady, the hours fly.
I'll help you across the street . . . Good bye.

(Recitation to accompany song, "Little Old Lady")

DO IT TODAY

This putting off things till tomorrow —
Do you do it? . . . or you? . . . or do you?
This waiting till later . . . you know what?
It's a rather unwise thing to do.

These kind words that need to be spoken —
This helping hand that we should give —
Yes, there IS tomorrow, I grant you,
But TODAY is the day that we live.

Yes, really, today is the only —
The only day anyone lives.
The yesterdays gave us their mem'ries;
And tomorrow, our hope to us gives.

But TODAY . . . It's the last time we'll have it.
This one will soon sink in the west . . .
This brick for our house of tomorrow . . .
Have we made it strong for the test?

There's really no time for vacations.
You can't build a house that is strong,
If some of the bricks you put in it
Are weak or are soft or are wrong.

So, fellows and girls, if you'll let me
Just give this advice —if I may —
Get in with the gang that is building
The bricks for tomorrow TODAY.

It's the only real way to be happy,
And you want to be happy, I know.
So get in with the kids building real bricks
From today for tomorrow! Let's go!

(Recitation to accompany original song, "Do It Today")

WHERE HAS THE SUMMER GONE?

It seems 'twas only yesterday
Life's Spring was in the air,
And all the dreams of youth,
Like sunshine, falling on my hair.

And all the charm of golden days
In such profusion came,
I had no time to think they would
Not always be the same.

I filled the garden of my heart
With flowers of brilliant hue,
Without a pause — without a thought
Of what the frost would do.

I loitered in the luxury
Of Life's warm Summer sun;
And loved beneath the Summer moon
After the day was done.

And little feet came pattering
Beside my garden wall,
With little rosebuds to be kissed
Whenever I should call.

And in my willows, robins came
To build a nest like mine.
And they, too, sang their hearts away —
Drunk with the Summer's wine.

But now the moon and sun are cold —
Robins and roses gone.
The little feet are far away,
And frost is on the dawn.

And, in my heart, a chill more deep,
For now, at last, I know:
Summer has gone and, near at hand,
Life's winter and the snow.

(Recitation for original song of same title)

MAN'S STRUGGLE TO UNBALANCE NATURE

Through all of the ages, Mother Nature has kept a very critical eye on what we call "balance in nature." All living things, plants and animals, insects, microbes — all living things are subject to a regulation of their population to keep nature in that balance. You have heard some of the serious reports of the army worm infestation in many of the states and counties. It is obvious that if all of these army worms were permitted to mature and reproduce and live on, within a few years they would be so numerous that all plant life would disappear. Mother Nature has not yet allowed one of her species to so unbalance her scheme of things and very likely never will. In fact, already in Indiana and Ohio, entomologists are observing insect parasites which are coming to cut back the excessive population of army worms. It is a parasitic fly which lays its eggs on the backs of the worms. The egg hatches, then lives as a maggot inside the army worm until it is killed. And so, nature's servants are already at work keeping her inevitable balance.

This year's infestation of the seventeen-year locusts, or periodical cicadas, too, is about to be cut back. As the female cicada sits on a limb depositing hundreds of eggs in small holes which she drills in the bark, a tink midge fly waits and watches. As the cicada moves on, the little fly follows her path and deposits just one tiny egg in most of the cicada's egg holes. Before the cicada eggs hatch, the tiny midge egg will emerge and soon will be thriving on a fine diet of baby cicadas — so serving to help nature keep its balance. Even as the corn borer has its parasitic lydella fly, waiting beside every living thing is its own specially prepared parasite, insect pest or disease, by which Mother Nature may retain her organization, and each specie retain its opportunity to compete for life.

It is not necessarily the strongest that wins in the competition to survive, however. It is the individual which most successfully adjusts itself to its environment. The great and powerful dinosaur, as much as sixty feet long, and weighing tons, might possibly have done fine in the steaming, prehistoric swamps, had it not been for the tiny little animal, no bigger than a terrier, which lived off dinosaur eggs, left unprotected by their mother. And so, the dinosaur took its place with the other failures.

From the very short space of time that mankind has lived on the earth, he has been a parasite on nature. He has lived on plants that grew on the soil, and from the animals that ate those plants. He has done well as a parasite of nature's wealth. In recent years, he has done doubly well, because by the use of his extraordinary, imaginative, inventive and comprehensive brain, he has succeeded in protecting himself from many of the culling devices Mother Nature had in store for him. The wild beasts of the forests, and the poisonous reptiles and insects no longer cut down his population. Man kills them first. He has domesticated plants, and learned to till the soil so he is less dependent upon nature's very slow agriculture for his plant food. He has bred and trained and selected animals to a prodigious capacity for the production of animal food in the form of meats, eggs, milk, and other products. He boasts of conquering nature and bringing her under his domination, through the great power of his thinking mind!

He has placed within his own hands chemicals to kill weeds which would compete with his domesticated crops, chemicals to kill insects that attack his domesticated animals or crops, and chemicals that will protect them from, or save them from, disease.

He has learned a little about sanitation to protect himself from filth-borne diseases. He has learned immunization and vaccination as a defense against other diseases. He has surrounded himself with specialists in fighting disease, and these specialists in turn have equipped themselves with an amazing array of medicines and tools and techniques to defend him from disease and death.

Thus, surrounded by the creations of his own master-mind, man is succeeding amazingly in holding back and distorting the plans of old Mother Nature. Like a locust scourge, or like the rabbits of Australia, man is multiplying.

The great scientists of the world are looking at this phenomenon of increasing human population with growing concern. They know that never in history of life on earth has a specie succeeded for long, if it continues to be such an enemy of all other life about it. These same scientists look with horror at the destruction which is taking place in our soil as mankind bleeds that kind soil to death with his unnatural domesticated plants, stimulated with chemicals, and protected from Mother Nature's culling hook by his chemical sprays and all. And to cap the depredations of this greatest parasite that nature has ever seen, man strips the soil of its cover and leaves it open to the very same clawing fingers of weather which, only a few centuries ago, tore down most of the mountains of the world and spread their debris in the level places so that plants could grow and there could be life on the earth. But this time, that very life-giving stuff of the soil is being carried away to be lost in the sea — the sea which can keep and restore *its* natural balance because mankind is unable to infest it!

If we were to compare the age of the earth with one year, mankind has been upon it less than a day. The white man has been in North America only seven seconds and during the last four seconds of that time, the wildness of his destructiveness has reached such heights as the world has never known. The question is: "Can it last? Can man continue to protect himself from Mother Nature's determination to keep her balance?" The answer, there can be no doubt, is an unquestionable "No!" She will find a way, as she always has — in fact, she is finding ways already.

Man, as well as his domesticated crops and animals, is being attacked every year by new diseases and pests. War, which is a national mental disease, and just as truly a disease as cancer or tuberculosis, has been increasing since the turn of the century. All about us we see a weakening of the vital fibre as indicated in the deterioration of our homes, the crowding of our children into inadequate schools, and relaxing vigilance and interest in so fundamentally an essential thing as the *keeping* of health. The rough and beautiful, brown hand of old Mother Nature is writing on the wall — no, writing in the gullying soil! — and those who are wise will read it soon and prepare to save themsleves by working with and not against Nature's immutable laws.

Here is a story. A frightful parallel to man's struggle to unbalance Nature. In the highlands of the great central mountain chain in Norway and Sweden, there is a little animal called the Lemming, a harmless little chap which lives on grass roots and stalks, shoots of dwarf birch, and reindeer lichens and mosses. From time to time, however, a reproduction explosion occurs in the lemming population, and at those times, countless herds of them advance steadily and slowly, disregarding all obstacles, down across the farm lands, leaving only devastation in their wake. But as they go, all nature turns against them as they have turned against nature. The beasts and birds of prey follow them, and even domestic animals join in stamping them into the ground with their feet, and even eating their bodies. During their mad journey, epidemic disease breaks out among them called "lemming fever" (probably a form of tularemia, and thousands die. But on they go, probably laughing to themselves, congratulating themselves on having conquered old Mother Nature. None ever return. Onward and onward they march, those that survive, until they reach the sea. Into it they plunge, swim out, and all are drowned! Now, they do not swim out into the sea to commit suicide; rather, they have come across rivers and lakes, on that treacherous journey down from the mountains, and each one may say to himself: "I have never been drowned! Let's go on to larger fields!" Just as Americans say: "The United States has never lost a war!", or our health magazines tell us we are getting healthier all the time and there is nothing to worry about.

Be assured, there is much to worry about. We had better go about making friends with old Mother Nature, learning her way, following the rules she has laid down. Otherwise, we may very well find ourselves in the company of the dinosaur, the sabre-toothed tiger, and the other misfits who failed to learn that Mother Nature's laws are to be obeyed.

SHOW'S END

Like ships that pass upon the boundless sea,
  We meet and cry, "Hail! Hail!" and then "Farewell,"
Then glide away across the pathless deep
  To fade forever where the sea meets sky.
Hail, passing wond'rer . . . and farewell!
    We sail uncharted seas for ports unknown —
    May friendly winds swell full your sails with joy!
May you fair wisdom for a pilot take!
    May you be steadfast to the love you claim.
And may you, someday, drop your anchor down
  In a safe port of everlasting peace.

GO NOW, LITTLE BOOK

Go now, Little Book. You have much work to do.
It is work that I can't do myself.
And you've failed in your task if your page is not read
And you just gather dust on the shelf.

    You have thoughts to deliver and loves to inspire —
    A challenge more richly to live —
    A chuckle, perhaps, and a question to ask,
    The answer to which I can't give.

I hope, Little Book, you'll be passed all around
Until you are tattered and worn —
That you lift just a little, because you are there,
The burdens that have to be borne.

    Talk to ears that can hear and to hearts that can feel,
    And t oeyes, as you help them to see.
    Then your work will be done and our goal will be won,
    Little Book. For you really are me.

INDEX OF TITLES

Set in Linotype Antique *and italic*

by The Casey Print Shop, Andrews, Indiana 46702